Different and Better | *The Spirit of Andersen —* **1903–2003**

differ

The Spirit of Andersen

entrance

1903 — 2003

Andersen Corporation — Bayport, Minnesota — United States

©2004 Andersen Corporation
100 Fourth Avenue North
Bayport, Minnesota
55003

All Rights Reserved

ISBN : 0-9743833-0-9

Library of Congress Control
Number: 2003096752

Front Endsheet Image
This image depicts a coding
system used to track productivity
in production. Each color
represents a different employee's work. A similar system
based on the same principles
is in use today.
Charissa Uemura – Photo

Rear Endsheet Image
Printed on the rear endsheet is
an image of the Fibrex material
currently used in many new
products in its raw pellet state.

Typography and House
Mrs. Eaves Family – *Emigre*
Meta Family – *FontShop*
Serifa Family – *Adobe*

Paper
135gr GardaPat 13 Woodfree
Archival Coated Matte Text,
Made to ISO Standards 9706

Cloth
Brill Calandre Black

Headbands
Guth & Wolf Farbkarte #17

**Concept Development
and Research**
Craig Davidson and Jack El-Hai

Writing and Editorial
Jack El-Hai – Minneapolis

Editorial Direction
Maureen McDonough
Stacy Einck

Book Design
Craig Davidson for
Civic Design – Minneapolis

Design Consultant
Jeanne Lee for
Jeanne Lee Design – Minneapolis

Studio Photography
Paul Schell for Clearsite
New Media – Faribault, MN

Index Development
Stephanie Reymann

Prepress, Printing and Bindery
Oddi Printing – Reykjavik,
Iceland

Contents

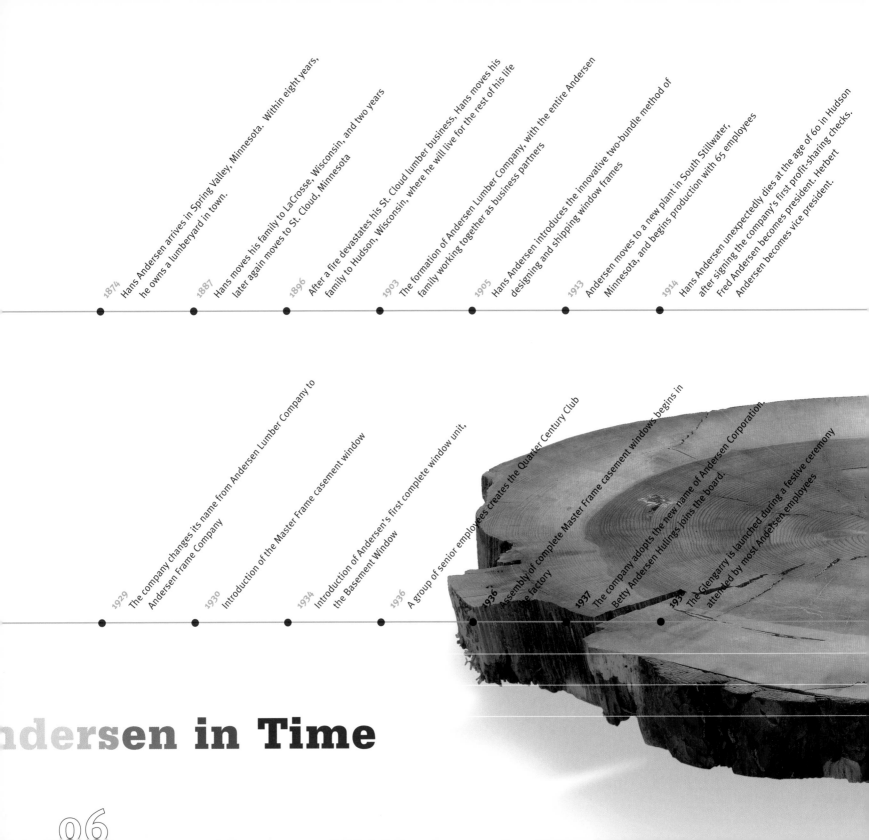

1874 Hans Andersen arrives in Spring Valley, Minnesota. Within eight years, he owns a lumberyard in town.

1887 Hans moves his family to LaCrosse, Wisconsin, and two years later again moves to St. Cloud, Minnesota

1896 After a fire devastates his St. Cloud lumber business, Hans moves his family to Hudson, Wisconsin, where he will live for the rest of his life

1903 The formation of Andersen Lumber Company, with the entire Andersen family working together as business partners

1905 Hans Andersen introduces the innovative two-bundle method of designing and shipping window frames

1913 Andersen moves to a new plant in South Stillwater, Minnesota, and begins production with 65 employees

1914 Hans Andersen unexpectedly dies at the age of 60 in Hudson after signing the company's first profit-sharing checks. Fred Andersen becomes president. Herbert Andersen becomes vice president.

1929 The company changes its name from Andersen Lumber Company to Andersen Frame Company

1930 Introduction of the Master Frame casement window

1934 Introduction of Andersen's first complete window unit, the Basement Window

1936 A group of senior employees creates the Quarter Century Club

1936 Assembly of complete Master Frame casement windows begins in the factory

1937 The company adopts the new name of Andersen Corporation. Betty Andersen Hulings joins the board.

193 The Glengarry is launched during a festive ceremony attended by most Andersen employees

ndersen in Time

06

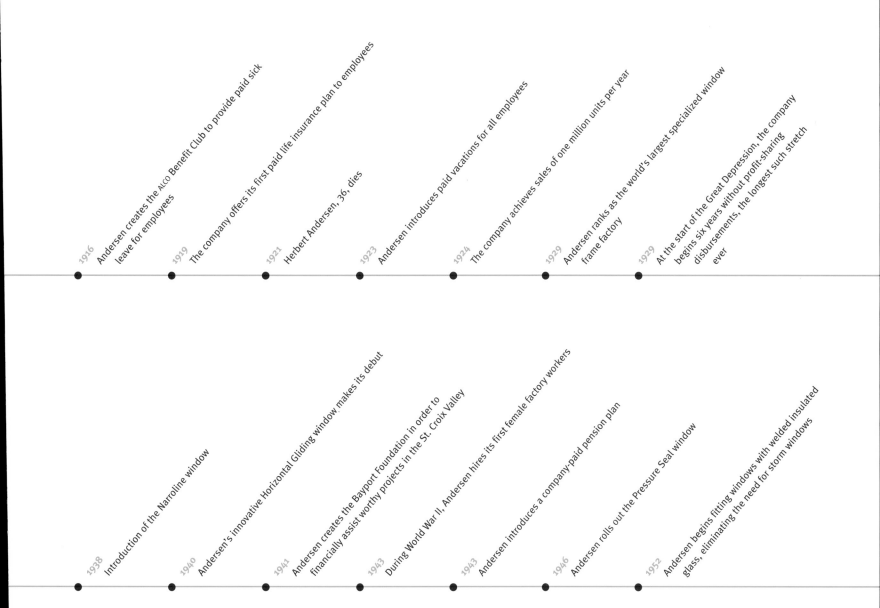

1916   Andersen creates the ALCO Benefit Club to provide paid sick leave for employees

1919   The company offers its first paid life insurance plan to employees

1921   Herbert Andersen, 36, dies

1923   Andersen introduces paid vacations for all employees

1924   The company achieves sales of one million units per year

1929   Andersen ranks as the world's largest specialized window frame factory

1929   At the start of the Great Depression, the company begins six years without profit-sharing disbursements, the longest such stretch ever

1938   Introduction of the Narroline window

1940   Andersen's innovative Horizontal Gliding window makes its debut

1941   Andersen creates the Bayport Foundation in order to financially assist worthy projects in the St. Croix Valley

1943   During World War II, Andersen hires its first female factory workers

1943   Andersen introduces a company-paid pension plan

1946   Andersen rolls out the Pressure Seal window

1952   Andersen begins fitting windows with welded insulated glass, eliminating the need for storm windows

07

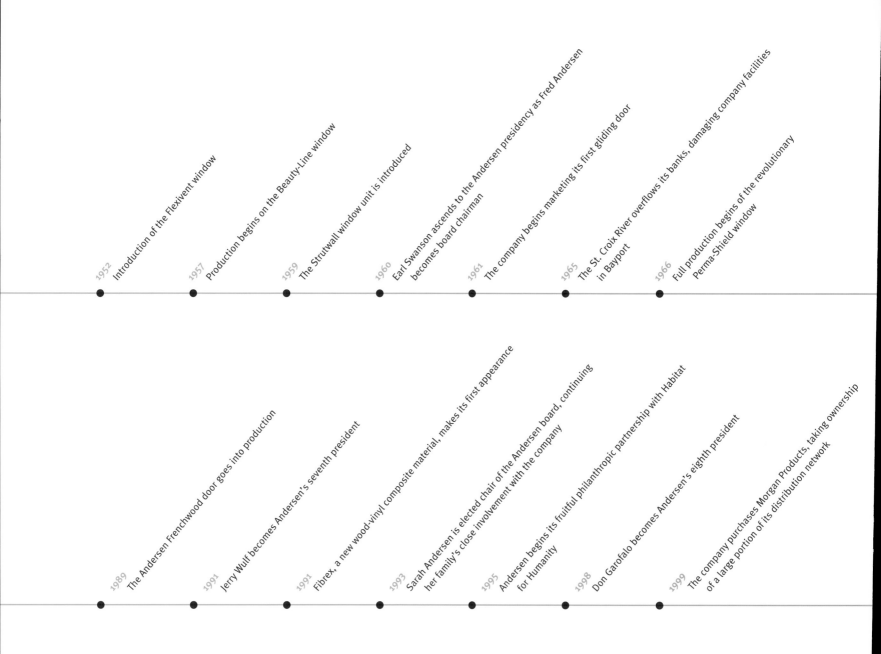

1952 Introduction of the Flexivent window

1957 Production begins on the Beauty-Line window

1959 The Strutwall window unit is introduced

1960 Earl Swanson ascends to the Andersen presidency as Fred Andersen becomes board chairman

1961 The company begins marketing its first gliding door

1965 The St. Croix River overflows its banks, damaging company facilities in Bayport

1966 Full production begins of the revolutionary Perma-Shield window

1989 The Andersen Frenchwood door goes into production

1991 Jerry Wulf becomes Andersen's seventh president

1991 Fibrex, a new wood-vinyl composite material, makes its first appearance

1993 Sarah Andersen is elected chair of the Andersen board, continuing her family's close involvement with the company

1995 Andersen begins its fruitful philanthropic partnership with Habitat for Humanity

1998 Don Garofalo becomes Andersen's eighth president

1999 The company purchases Morgan Products, taking ownership of a large portion of its distribution network

08

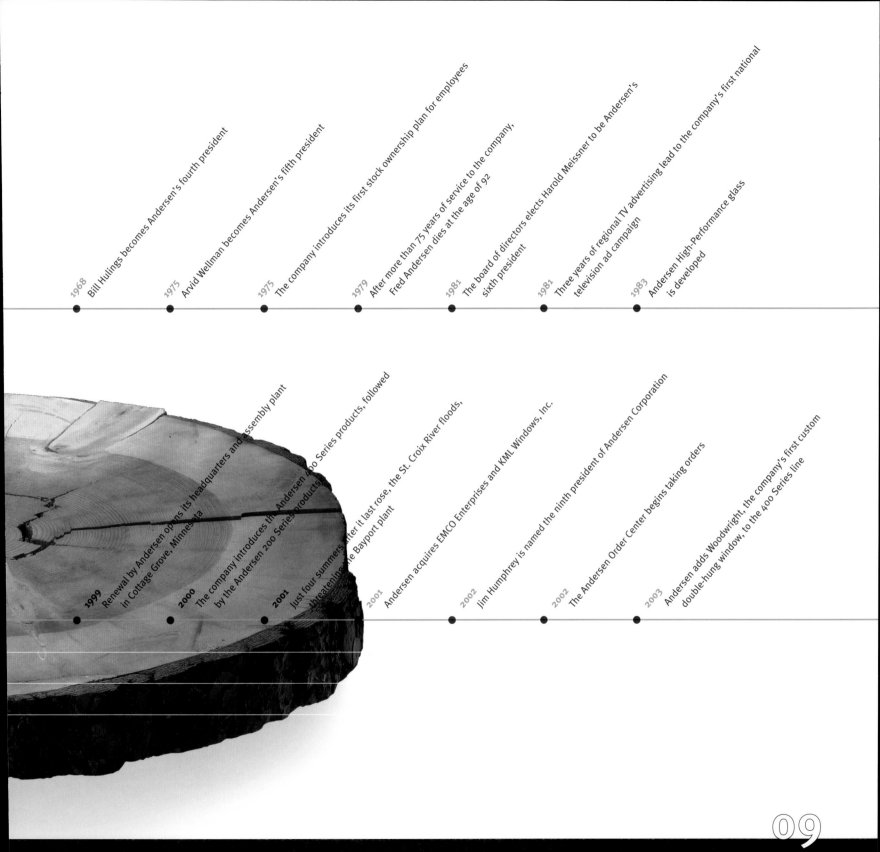

1968 Bill Hulings becomes Andersen's fourth president

1975 Arvid Wellman becomes Andersen's fifth president

1975 The company introduces its first stock ownership plan for employees

1979 After more than 75 years of service to the company, Fred Andersen dies at the age of 92

1981 The board of directors elects Harold Meissner to be Andersen's sixth president

1981 Three years of regional TV advertising lead to the company's first national television ad campaign

1983 Andersen High-Performance glass is developed

1999 Renewal by Andersen opens its headquarters and assembly plant in Cottage Grove, Minnesota

2000 The company introduces the Andersen 400 Series products, followed by the Andersen 200 Series products

2001 Just four summers after it last rose, the St. Croix River floods, threatening the Bayport plant

2001 Andersen acquires EMCO Enterprises and KML Windows, Inc.

2002 Jim Humphrey is named the ninth president of Andersen Corporation

2002 The Andersen Order Center begins taking orders

2003 Andersen adds Woodwright, the company's first custom double-hung window, to the 400 Series line

09

Introduction

As we celebrate our Centennial, it is important to understand how and why Andersen became the great company that it is today — to capture the spirit of Andersen. In this book, we pay respect to the people whose labor, wisdom and commitment built the window business in times of opportunity and weathered the company through times of lackluster performance and hardship. We also document what we've learned over the years so that we can apply it to keep this company great for another 100 years.

When I reflect upon Andersen's history, I believe two forces had the greatest influence on the company we have become — innovation and people.

As a result of a longstanding commitment to innovation — to being "different and better" — Andersen has made an indelible mark on the industry, the business and the communities in which we live and work. Beautiful and enduring products are just part of the story. On these pages you'll read about ingenuity in manufacturing, research and technology, sales, marketing, distribution, human resources, business models and business practices.

Andersen innovation — new ideas, new technologies, and new solutions — has been the driving force for our success over the years. It has given us the ability to reinvent ourselves time and time again to meet the needs of a changing marketplace. It is what has made us an industry leader.

But this innovation did not happen all by itself — it occurred because of the talented and committed people who have been part of the Andersen "family" for 100 years. That brings me to the second of the two greatest influences on Andersen's success — its people.

We are grateful to our founder, Hans J. Andersen, for the principles he established in **1903** that continue to guide us today. Hire the best people. Expect them to do exceptional work. Treat them with respect. Share success.

These principles have had a lasting impact on all of us and have been remarkably enduring in our culture. One hundred years later, we still believe in working "all together" toward a common purpose. The concept of partnership is one of the values that we hold dear — along with excellence, integrity, innovation and corporate citizenship. These values are the spirit of Andersen. They speak to our past and they guide our future. They are what make us Andersen. If we continue to live by these values, I know our future will be even brighter in the next 100 years.

Don Garofalo

Chief Executive Officer

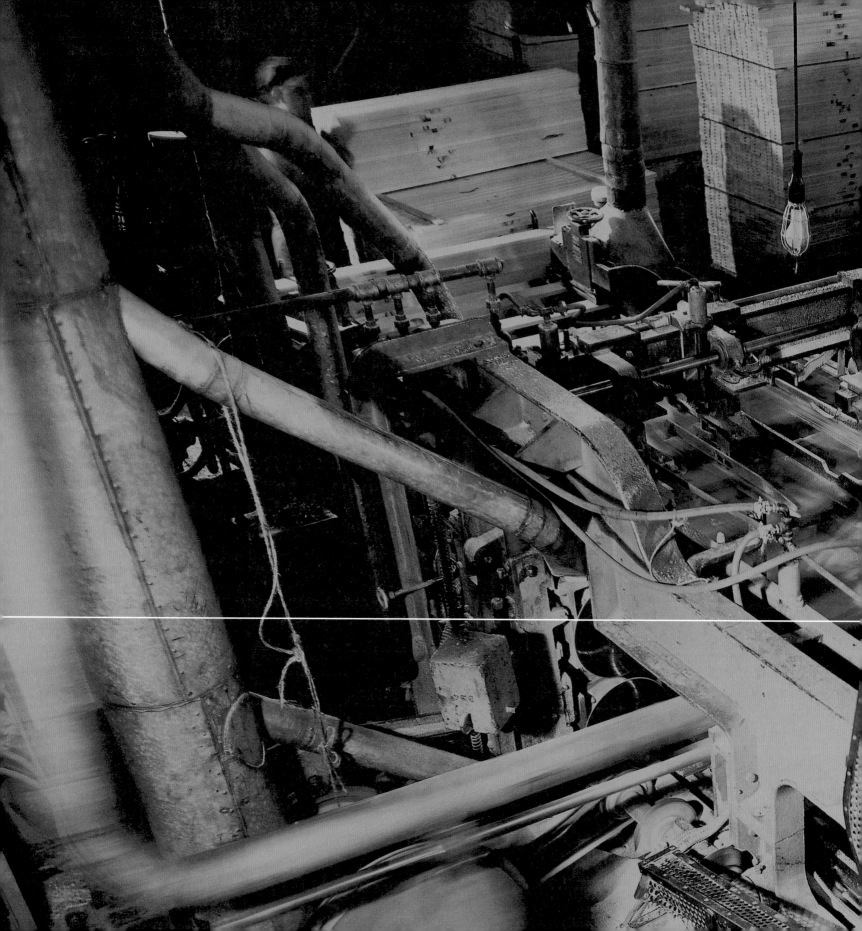

Innovation

13

"WHAT CAN WE DO BETTER?" —Fred Andersen

14

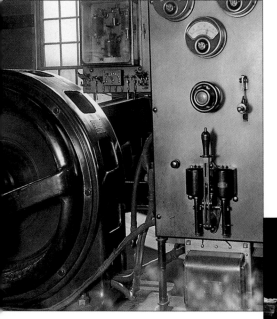

15

innovation

16

innovation

Community

In a geographic sense, Andersen's home communities are scattered across North America. But to look at the dots on a map and imagine that they alone convey the importance of **community** in the history of Andersen Corporation is a mistake. From its first year of operation, when Hans Andersen gathered together his family and a small group of employees in an effort to build a new business, Andersen has survived and thrived through the efforts of its many communities. The company does have important communities based on geographic closeness, but many of the company's greatest successes have originated with the formation of communities anchored by other commonalities: the recognition of new opportunities, the appreciation of common values, and, most of all, the shared purpose of giving customers the products and services they need. Andersen Corporation manufactures windows and doors, but one should not overlook how successful the company has also been at community-building, the process of uniting people behind some common purpose. In this chapter we examine that process, starting with the ways, even before the company's actual birth, several communities contributed to the character Andersen Corporation would eventually assume and the direction it would take.

Spring Valley, Minnesota

Clustered around Minnesota State Highway 63 in southern Minnesota, about 115 miles south of Minneapolis–St. Paul and not far from the Iowa state line, is a prosperous town of 2,500 people. Spring Valley, situated on the prairie but within sight of a gorgeous hardwood forest, is one of the communities closest to Andersen's heart, even though its role in the company's history predates by years the actual establishment of the Corporation. In Spring Valley company founder Hans Jacob Andersen made his first true home in America, courted a bride, began his family, and started his life as an entrepreneur and businessman.

Hans, a Danish immigrant, arrived in Spring Valley in **1874** at the age of 19 or 20, after two years spent felling trees and clearing fields in the eastern United States, and laying brick in Chicago. Eager to set down his toolbox in a non-Danish town where he could improve his English, Hans made a lucky decision to settle in Spring Valley. He soon met a school teacher named Mary Kezia Cummings, a pale and delicately featured member of one of the town's oldest families, and they were married in **1881**. They had three children, Mary, Herbert, and Fred, when Mary Cummings Andersen died in childbirth in **1891**. In the years that followed, Hans remarried and, in **1903**, the entire family would join forces to launch the business that grew into the Andersen Corporation.

As Hans' family enlarged in Spring Valley, so did his work prospects. Known to his neighbors as "Jake" Andersen, he started a construction business and by **1882** owned a lumberyard. Advertising himself as a contractor, architect, and dealer of building materials, he designed and erected several of Spring Valley's most important buildings, including the Methodist Episcopal Church (which still stands and is listed on the National Register of Historic Places) and the Andersen Opera House.

In **1887** Hans purchased a lumber wholesale company in LaCrosse, Wisconsin, and moved his family there. Two years later the Andersens again moved to St. Cloud, Minnesota, where Hans operated a sawmill. His wife Mary Cummings Andersen died there in **1891**. "Her many friends have been stricken with grief by the sudden announcement of her death," the Spring Valley newspaper reported, "and sympathize with the bereaved husband and children." Her remains were laid to rest in the cemetery at Spring Valley, the town in which she spent most of her life.

Hans remained involved in the Spring Valley community as owner of the lumberyard and opera house until the early-**1890s**. The town had transformed him from raw immigrant to husband, father, builder, and business leader.

20

3

Broadway Looking North, Spring Valley, Minn.

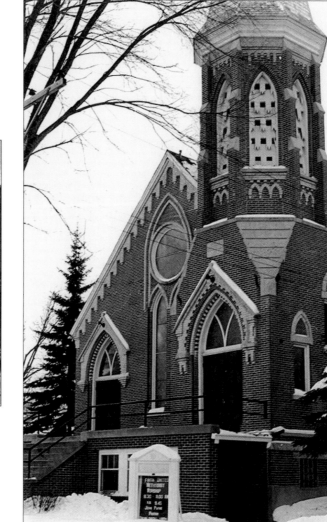

4

21

1. Spring Valley Land Promotion
In 1907, more than 30 years after Hans Andersen's arrival in the young community, plenty of Spring Valley farm land was still available for purchase.

2. Spring Valley Rail Depot
The railroad station in Spring Valley, pictured in 1910.

3. Broadway, Spring Valley
The community's main thoroughfare, circa 1900.

4. Spring Valley Methodist Episcopal Church
Designed and built by Hans Andersen, this local landmark is listed in the National Register of Historic Places.

community

Hudson, Wisconsin

Fortune treated Hans Andersen roughly during the years immediately after his departure from Spring Valley. He lost his wife Mary Cummings Andersen after just ten years of marriage, took sole charge of their three young children, and, as owner of a sawmill in St. Cloud, Minnesota, fell victim to a combination of fire and economic depression that wiped out his business and his personal fortune. With his second wife, Sarah "Sadie" McDonald Andersen, whom Hans married in **1896**, he rebuilt his life in Hudson, Wisconsin, a community on the east bank of the St. Croix River, which divides Minnesota from Wisconsin. For decades, the river had served as an immense highway for the region's lumber industry, the route by which logs cut from the seemingly inexhaustible forests of upper Minnesota and Wisconsin floated south to scores of sawmills and lumberyards.

Hans' comeback as a businessman began in **1896**, when he moved his family to Hudson and scraped up every available dollar in order to buy millions of board feet of logs and lumber that the previous owners could not convey across the unsafe ice surface of the St. Croix River to the nearest railroad depot in Afton, Minnesota. Hans studied the capricious currents beneath the river ice, laid out the longest timbers as a temporary bridge over the frozen surface, and skidded the lumber across to the opposite bank before the arrival of spring broke up the ice.

This incredible undertaking restored Hans' confidence and financial reserves. For the next 17 years, Hudson was his home base. He took on the management of a sawmill and opened a retail lumberyard called the Wisconsin Lumber and Building Company. Then, in **1903**, he started a window-frame manufacturing business in Hudson with his family. That enterprise grew beyond all of their dreams into what we now know as the Andersen Corporation.

Hudson became the Andersens' community in more than just a business sense. Hans threw himself into the civic and social life of the town.

When Hans died suddenly in **1914**, the people of Hudson felt shock and great sadness. The *Hudson Star-Observer* reported that "practically the whole city attended the services" in the town's Presbyterian Church. "While he could not be classed with the pioneers of this community, his life has been so active and his services so great, during the years that he has been among us that we had come to look upon him as an indispensable factor in every business and social enterprise.... His fertile mind seemed always at work and most of the undertakings of the city and community for many years bear the imprint of his ready hand," the newspaper eulogized. Hans was buried in Hudson's Willow River Cemetery.

His widow, Sarah McDonald Andersen, remained a part of the community fabric for another two decades. She lived in Hudson until her death in **1934**.

22

2

3

abril 1905

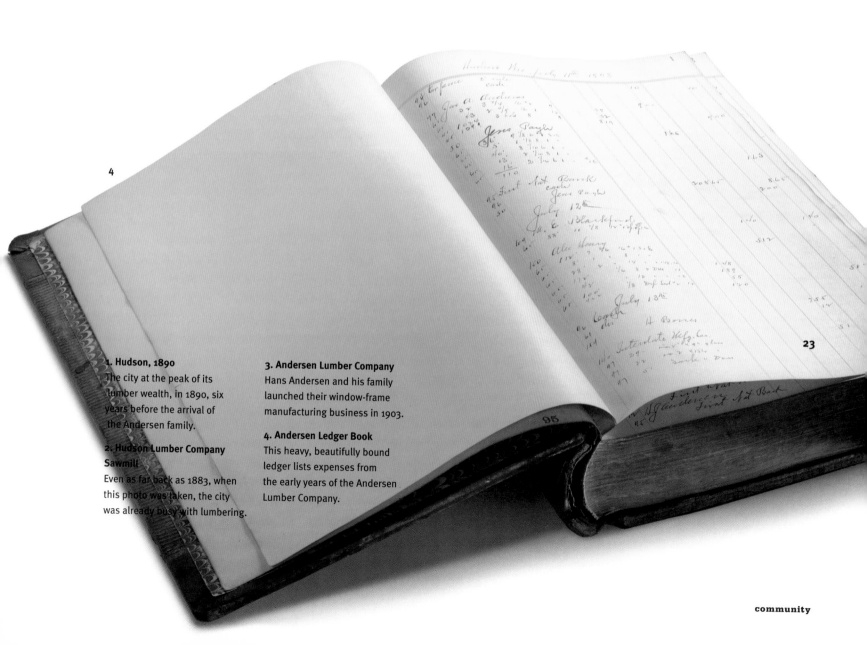

4

95

23

1. Hudson, 1890
The city at the peak of its lumber wealth, in 1890, six years before the arrival of the Andersen family.

2. Hudson Lumber Company Sawmill
Even as far back as 1883, when this photo was taken, the city was already busy with lumbering.

3. Andersen Lumber Company
Hans Andersen and his family launched their window-frame manufacturing business in 1903.

4. Andersen Ledger Book
This heavy, beautifully bound ledger lists expenses from the early years of the Andersen Lumber Company.

Bayport, Minnesota

Who can imagine what Andersen would be without Bayport, or what Bayport would be without Andersen? For nearly a century the company and the city have led blended lives, forming an intertwined community in which each helps the other.

Andersen began the relationship in **1912** when the company — bursting from its cramped Hudson factory because of a surge of new business — bought a large tract of land on the Minnesota bank of the St. Croix River, three miles upstream from Hudson. Three railroads served the site, as opposed to the one that ran through Hudson. Hans, Herbert, and Fred Andersen planned to build a much larger factory on this land, which lay within the boundaries of an unassuming community called South Stillwater.

Formed by the merger of the towns of Bangor, Baytown, and Middletown, South Stillwater had long associations with the lumber trade. Its first sawmill was built in **1852**.

Without Andersen, South Stillwater might have turned inward following the decline of the Upper Midwest's timber industry, becoming a small river community with a few businesses and a handful of homes. Instead, it was reborn as Bayport (the name was officially changed in **1922** to declare independence from the neighboring town of Stillwater), a thriving business and manufacturing center. Andersen's adoption of the St. Croix Valley as its home helped in the following years to draw many new manufacturing concerns.

Bayport gave Andersen a great deal in return. The city had, and still has, a neighborly spirit and tranquility that are rare — qualities that complement Andersen's own priorities on working together and dedication to quality. Unlike some other river communities that prospered during the boom times of the Logging Era, Bayport did not live in its past, and it adapted itself to the busy window-frame concern that would eventually become the enormous Andersen Corporation. The town's stability has contributed to the traditional steadiness of the company's workforce.

There has been so much give and take in the ongoing relationship between Bayport and Andersen, it's impossible to know which has benefitted more. Bayport has given Andersen many prized associations with local business partners, including Bayport Printing Company, which has produced printed materials for Andersen since **1913**, and Pawnee's (now known as Woody's), the Bayport watering hole that for more than 75 years has been an after-hours gathering spot for Andersen workers, provided a home for ALCO bowling tournaments, and supplied refreshments for company parties and events.

24

PEOPLE REALLY
Live
IN BAYPORT

Bayport, Minnesota, a town of homes and churches and schools and playgrounds and thriving businesses, located in the "Friendly Valley" of the St. Croix River on the border between Minnesota and Wisconsin.

Andersen Corporation, its affiliated foundations, and the Andersen family have, in turn, strengthened Bayport. Since it opened the factory in 1913, the company has provided employee volunteers for Bayport's volunteer fire department. Andersen founded the Bayport Home Company, which built and helped Andersen employees and other Bayport residents buy affordable housing in town. (The first property offered, a five-room house, sold for $4,000 in 1924.) Andersen provided the impetus behind the community's first financial institution, the First State Bank and Trust. The Andersen community — including the company's Bayport Foundation, the founding family, and other grateful company officers — helped finance the town's library, school, municipal buildings, parks, Stillwater's Lakeview hospital, and many other vital functions, all without intruding in the town's operations or leaving Bayport a dependent "company town."

No connection between a firm and its hometown is perfect, and inevitably over nearly 100 years there have been ups and downs in Andersen's relationship with its Bayport neighbors. But that Bayport today retains its unassuming, friendly personality, and that Andersen has blossomed in this environment into one of the world's leading building-materials manufacturers, are both evidence of the community partnership that the town and corporation have nurtured since 1913.

25

1, 3. Bayport Promotional Brochure
This brochure was developed in the mid-1950s to highlight life in the "Friendly Valley."

2. Bayport
This photo was taken before 1922, when the city's name was changed from South Stillwater. The Andersen plant and its tower are visible in the distance.

1

5

2

3

4

26

The White Pine Inn

On June 1, **1925**, the down-beat of an orchestra conductor's baton introduced the world to the White Pine Inn, Bayport's first hotel. Visitors touring the Inn, which was located in the town's compact business district, took in the colonial architecture, the lobby paneled completely in white pine, the massive pine table in the dining room, the solid pine doors hung on wrought iron hinges, and the ceilings striped with white pine beams. Room rates began at $1.50 a night, and the dining room served breakfasts at 20 cents, lunches at 60 cents, and dinners — the chicken and trout as specialties — at 85 cents. The manager, Thor Follestad, who had previously been assistant manager of the Leamington Hotel in Minneapolis, proudly officiated.

Andersen financed this enterprise, partly as a promotion for the wood from which the company made its window frames. Mostly, however, President Fred Andersen believed that Bayport needed a well-run hotel for business guests and other visitors to the city. In 1926 the Inn hosted Andersen's first sales conference for the company's distributors. Arriving from 14 states aboard a chartered Pullman sleeping car, the 36 participants saw white pine on their tours of the Andersen factory and in their rooms.

6

7

Eventually Andersen sold the hotel. The restaurant gained a reputation as one of Minnesota's finest.

The building underwent another change of ownership and transformation in 1990, when the four Andersen-related foundations funded a thorough remodeling that made it the new home of the Bayport Public Library.

The old White Pine Inn continues to serve the community, although in ways that Fred Andersen and his contemporaries couldn't have anticipated.

1. Bayport Printing Company

One of Andersen's oldest suppliers in the city, Bayport's largest printer is pictured here around 1925.

2-4. The White Pine Inn

Andersen built the White Pine Inn in 1925 to give Bayport its first large lodging house. The pine, a symbol of the company's trademark building material, was inescapable throughout the inn.

5-6. Filling Station and Ballfield

By the mid-20th-century, Bayport was a bustling community with its full share of autos needing service and players — including Andersen employees — in need of a baseball diamond.

7. Andersen House

The longtime home of Fred and Kitty Andersen is now a restored jewel, a company meeting center that retains the spirit of its former owners.

community

New Communities

Starting in the **1990s**, the company has brought new communities into the Andersen Corporation fold by opening new factories and acquiring other companies. These cities with their own rich histories now work in partnership with Andersen, just as others have inspired and shaped the company in the past.

Centralia, Ontario
The home of Dashwood Industries Limited, once a Perma-Shield licensee and now an Andersen subsidiary that produces roof windows, Centralia lies in one of Canada's most agriculturally rich regions. It is a small community located near the shore of Lake Huron.

Cottage Grove, Minnesota
Since **1999** Cottage Grove

has been home to the headquarters and assembly plant of Renewal by Andersen Corporation, the corporation's business devoted to replacing windows. Renewal by Andersen was launched in **1995**. Located southeast of the Twin Cities, Cottage Grove has more than 30,000 residents and is one of the region's fastest-growing cities. Its history dates back to the **1840s**, when the villages of Langdon and Old

Cottage Grove combined. The community includes a rich variety of historic structures, including the Munger House, built in **1852**, which is one of the oldest continually occupied homes in Minnesota.

Des Moines, Iowa, and Luray, Virginia
These are the home communities of EMCO Enterprises, Inc., an Andersen subsidiary and the nation's largest

← 1

2

4

3

1-4. Andersen Communities
(From left) The 200-Series pro-
duction facility in Menomonie,
Wisconsin; EMCO's facilities in
Des Moines; the home of
Dashwood Industries in
Centralia, Ontario; and KML's
facilities in London, Ontario.

manufacturer of storm doors.
Luray, a 190-year old town
located in Virginia's fabled
Shenandoah Valley, is the seat
of Page County. It serves as
an important gateway to
Shenandoah National Park.
Des Moines, the capital of
Iowa, is a Midwestern center
of arts and cultural affairs,
business, and government. Its
metro population of nearly
500,000 people enjoys
excellent schools and one of
the nation's shortest average
commute times.

Menomonie, Wisconsin
In 1999 Andersen selected
Menomonie as the site of the
assembly plant for its new
mid-band 200 Series of windows and patio doors.
Covering 200,000 square
feet, the plant employs about
250 people. The company
chose Menomonie because of
its easy access to interstate
highways, its closeness to
Andersen's other operations,
and the area's strong pool
of skilled workers. Like many

of Andersen's other home
communities, Menomonie
is closely connected with the
lumber and building-materials industries. The city
opened its first lumber mill
more than 180 years ago and
was the headquarters of the
world's largest white pine
milling operation during the
1870s. Today Menomonie is
a progressive university city
with a distinctive collection of
homes and buildings dating
from the time when timber
was king.

**Strathroy and London,
Ontario**
KML Windows Inc., another
Andersen subsidiary,
manufactures specialty doors
and windows in these neighboring Canadian cities. With
a metropolitan area population of 412,000, London has
grown into the largest city in
Southwestern Ontario,
boasting miles of trails, acres
of parkland, and some of the
world's friendliest people.

community

Andersen at War

World War II broke out in 1939. America remained a neutral country for more than two years. The U.S. government soon began a steady buildup of the military, however, and Andersen stepped forward as an early supplier of the American preparation for war with Germany, Italy, and Japan.

The government's initial orders were for window units, starting with 2,800 Narroline windows needed for a military housing project in South Carolina. Traditional business fell into a rapid decline — an order of gliding windows purchased by Alcatraz Prison was an exception — as housing construction stalled. The company experimentally produced a line of furniture parts and built some cabinets for Montgomery Ward. "In short, we are making every effort to get any woodworking business into our plant that will keep us busy and we are certainly going to continue such efforts," President Fred Andersen wrote to employees.

Governmental restrictions on the use of critical war materials, which included many metals that the company used for glazing panels, screen frames, sash weights, and weather stripping, hampered Andersen's attempts to produce traditional products. Even steel measuring tapes became unavailable, and the company helped employees locate used tapes for sale.

Andersen responded to these wartime restrictions by designing and producing the remarkable Victory Window, introduced a few months after the attack on Pearl Harbor as a replacement for the Narroline, which eliminated 97 percent of critical materials and slashed the amount of metal used in producing a window. Metal sash weights, for example, were replaced by weights made out of a mix of concrete and iron ore aggregate. In addition, the Victory Window was more weather tight than government standards required.

At the same time, Andersen workers were beginning to join the ranks of the military. The company, which never asked the government for the work-related deferment of any employee, promised all who entered the military that they would retain seniority rights and continue to receive any profit sharing. More than 250 employees eventually went into the service, and the company listed their names in an Honor Roll plaque at the main entrance of the plant. In a letter he sent in 1943, Fred Andersen urged the service members to continue thinking of themselves as part of the Andersen family.

As these workers put their lives on the line, Andersen was responding to the national emergency by quickly transforming into a much different manufacturer than it had been before 1942. Windows shifted to the background as the government flooded the company with orders for wooden ammunition boxes, mainly for 30 and 50 caliber shells. Workers,

30

organized in three round-the-clock shifts for the first time in company history, devised ingenious ways to produce these boxes faster. In the past, ammunition boxes had always been laboriously painted with identifying information after their assembly. Andersen's technicians invented a way to print the markings on the box parts as they rode the assembly line before completion, saving much time.

Andersen workers in the military gleefully reported seeing these boxes all over the world, including in the Dutch East Indies and Hawaii. This isn't surprising, since Andersen manufactured more ammunition boxes during the war than any other supplier.

Andersen made another unusual contribution to the war effort. In September 1942, employees erected a starkly designed, hut-like structure on the tennis courts next to Andersen's office building. This was the company's first

1. "E" Award Ceremony
Earl Swanson took a break from his military service to speak at the Army-Navy "E" Award Ceremony of 1944, honoring Andersen for its production of high-quality supplies for the government.

2. "E" Award Card and Pin
All Andersen employees received recognition for their participation in Andersen's war effort.

3. Ammunition Box
All over the world during World War II, members of America's military used these ingeniously fabricated boxes, which won Andersen "E" Award recognition from the U.S. government.

completed Stout house, a temporary shelter created by William Stout, the designer of the Ford Tri-Motor airplane. The Army Air Corps had issued Andersen a contract for 850 of these houses to be used by service-men in Alaska. In the 30 days following the order, Andersen workers figured out how to cut, mill, paint, and assemble the units; tested the finished product; passed government inspection; and began shipping the houses. It was an exhausting, exhilarating month.

For the high quality and on-time delivery of its work, Andersen's employees — about one-quarter of them now women due to a shortage of male workers — received Army-Navy "E" Awards in 1944 and 1945, an honor given to fewer than 3 percent of the nation's war plants. Each employee received a pin and the company was given an "E" Award flag.

When the war at last ended in the summer of 1945, six Andersen employees had died in battle. The world was changed in many ways, and Andersen's business would be forever different. The company had produced more than 5 million items for the war effort, including ammunition boxes, tool kit boxes, drawers for Army repair trucks, and prefabricated houses. The flexibility and quickness that Andersen had learned as a war supplier, all unexpected results of the company's response to the national challenge, would serve it very well in the years ahead.

The First World War

Andersen was a young com-pany, just 11 years old, when World War I erupted in Europe. America entered the war in 1917, and Andersen stepped forward to contribute what it could.

Although building construc-tion almost completely stopped, Fred Andersen kept the plant running by securing orders from the U.S. govern-ment for 200,000 window

frames for barracks and other military buildings, plus thousands of target frames used in gunnery practice. The window frames were cruder than those Andersen normally produced, made from Norway pine. During the last few months of 1918, Andersen devoted its entire attention to the war effort, suspending normal business.

Perhaps the company's biggest contribution to the war came in giving up Fred Andersen, who was then running the business with his brother Herbert. Commissioned as an Army captain, Fred managed operations at a sawmill that manufactured wooden airplane parts. When he returned to Bayport after the end of the war, Fred brought with him Bud Bird,

a military co-worker who served Andersen for 20 years as manager of the Bayport plant.

The number of Andersen workers who served in the military during World War I is not known, but an employee named Hesley Jensen died in action. Bayport's American Legion Post is named in his honor.

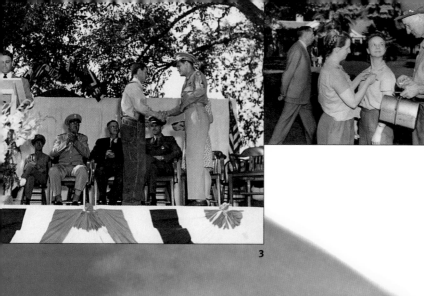

Special Edition

THE FRAME MAKER

BAYPORT, MINNESOTA   OCTOBER 1943

To Our Boys In The Armed Forces:

A Merry Christmas wherever you may be this Christmas Day!

We have 210 of our employees scattered all over the world and we have had no occasion to feel anything but the greatest pride in any man that has gone from our organization into this conflict.

Some of you are spending your second or third Christmas away from home, and, of course, for a good many of you this will be your first Christmas away from home.

I hope it will help you to have a worthwhile Christmas to know that we people here at home are proud of you and are sending you our very best wishes for a safe return before another Christmas rolls around. Also, please remember that you are members of our oganization and that we will be very happy to welcome you back when this war is over.

If in talking to your buddies you could say, "the organization to which I belong" rather than "the people for whom I used to work," in mentioning our company, it would indeed make us happy, and we hope it gives you a little feeling of security and happiness too, to think of yourselves as Andersen Corporation men on leave of absence.

Again to you all a Merry Christmas and God Bless You.

Yours very sincerely,

Fred C Andersen

1. Stout House
Andersen employees Jerry Hoppe, Earl Swanson, Stan Bull, and Gus Troden examine the first Stout House, which the company built for the U.S. military in 1942.

2. Receiving the "E" Award Flag
Fred Andersen (right) helped hold the flag that the company received from the government.

3. Employee Recognized at "E" Award Ceremony
Fred Andersen and Earl Swanson sat on stage as an Army-Navy representative congratulated an Andersen employee for his contributions to the war effort.

4. Applying the Pins
Bernice Wilson applied Ruth Radke's "E" Award pin as another Andersen employee looked on.

5. Special Holiday Issue of The *Frame Maker*
The front page of this issue of this 1943 company publication featured an open letter from Fred Andersen to the company's employees in the armed forces. "If in talking to your buddies you could say, 'the organization to which I belong' rather than 'the people for whom I used to work,' in mentioning our company, it would indeed make us happy, and we hope it gives you a little feeling of security and happiness too, to think of yourselves as Andersen Corporation men on leave of absence," Fred wrote.

The Glengarry

In 1938, a young man named Bob Berg heard that Fred Andersen was having a boat built for himself, and that he intended to cruise the boat along the St. Croix River and waterways beyond. "I asked Mrs. Betty Hulings if I could be the first applicant for cabin boy," Berg said. "I told her, 'I'd like to work on that.'" Fred hired Berg, beginning the young man's long relationship with one of the most colorful "corporate vehicles" in business history.

The *Glengarry*, as the boat is called, started its life at Dingle Boat Works of St. Paul, which built the hull and installed the engines. It then moved by truck to Bayport, where several Andersen millwrights, eager to stay busy during the Great Depression, helped complete it, building the helm, designing the cabinet work, and creating the windows, which, due to the boat's design, are all slightly out-of-square and different from one another in size. Fred christened the boat after a town in Canada in which his stepmother Sarah McDonald Andersen lived. (The town is named after a river valley in Scotland.)

On June 23, 1938, at a noon ceremony attended by most Andersen workers, Betty Andersen Hulings smashed a bottle of champagne against the hull, birthing the *Glengarry* into an existence that has brought pleasure to many of Andersen's employees, business partners, and community members. (According to retired employee Joe Judkins, Betty Andersen Hulings needed three swings of the magnum to achieve a satisfactory breakage of glass.) "Amid cheering and applause the *Glengarry* moved grandly out into the bay," the *Frame Maker* reported. Bob Berg was aboard for that maiden voyage. "We just went across the river and tied up for the afternoon," he says.

Berg said that the *Glengarry*, with a length of nearly 60 feet and its top speed often to twelve miles per hour, is not a difficult craft to handle, especially for someone like Fred Andersen, who had previous experience on the river as the occasional pilot of a launch the company used to deliver lumber to the opposite bank.

Four double guest rooms, two bathrooms, a galley, and a dining room made the *Glengarry* roomy and comfortable for extended cruises. Berg was along in 1939 when the boat made its first long trip, a 23-day, 1,600-mile excursion to Chicago and St. Louis via the St. Croix, Mississippi, Illinois, and Chicago rivers. Fred used the trip to meet with customers, tour river mills in Iowa, and attend a trade association meeting.

4

5

From the start, the *Glengarry* has been used to strengthen relationships with employees, business partners, and community organizations. Sixty to 70 trips per year for guests like these have been the general rule.

Berg left his plum job aboard the *Glengarry* to spend 30 years in the military. After he retired, "I kiddingly asked about having my old job back," he said. "In Bayport, saying something like that out loud is as good as broadcasting it. I got a call from Kitty Andersen [Fred's wife] saying, 'Bobby, a little bird said you wanted your old job back.' I became the *Glengarry*'s captain." He plied the currents of the St. Croix aboard the *Glengarry* for another 22 years.

Today, fully refurbished and gleaming, the *Glengarry* has been skippered since **1996** by Mark Wilmes. Don Madsen piloted it from **1950** to **1977**. For nearly two-thirds of the company's history, the boat has symbolized Andersen's ability to reach out to the community beautifully and proudly.

1. Proud Vessel
The Glengarry plies the waters of the St. Croix River in this watercolor painting.

2-3. Persistence Pays Off
Betty Andersen, foster-daughter of president Fred Andersen, had to try several times before successfully sending off the Glengarry with a bottle of champagne.

4. Community Connections
Excursions with scouting groups and other community organizations are common.

5. Ahoy
Today, Captain Mark Wilmes keeps the *Glengarry* in ship shape.

6. Glengarry Life Preserver

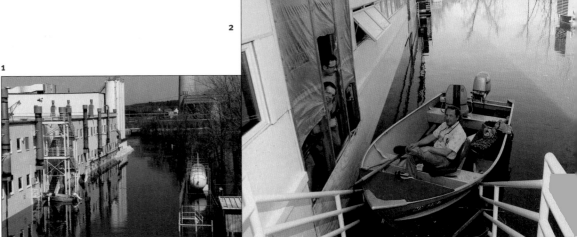

Floods

The years tick off irregularly, unpredictably: **1951**, **1952**, **1955**, **1965**, **1969**, **1997**, **2001**. Every so often, the St. Croix River, altered from its natural state by dams built in the **1940s**, makes a spring season memorable by overflowing its banks. When that happens, the communities along the river are reminded of nature's power.

Along with a chain of neighbors strung along the St. Croix, the Bayport plant sometimes suffers under this unstoppable rise of the water. The river's high water has forced the emergency removal of Andersen equipment, the rescue of company records, and the running of pumps night and day. Out in the lumberyard in **1965**, where the ground receded nearly four feet under the current, a huge amount of wood had to be carried to higher ground. Sales manager Jim Rowland spearheaded an effort, ultimately successful, to use Andersen's own switch engine to save 36 carloads of windows that were marooned on the railroad tracks. When the river returned to its channel, Andersen was stuck with a cleanup bill of about $50,000.

The overflow in **2001** engulfed the parking lot and forced the evacuation of valuables from the plant's basement. Even so, advance planning, including the building of a wall of more than 5000 sandbags, kept the plant open. Employees humorously placed alligator warning signs on the property. Andersen couldn't stop the water, but employees' decisive action ensured that the company would prevail over this challenge.

1. The Floods of 1997 and 2001
During the spring surges of the St. Croix River in 1997 and 2001, the water lapped the walls of the Andersen plant in Bayport and flooded the basement.

2. The Waters Rising
During the flood of 2001, employees inspected the east side of the building by boat. Some jokingly fished from the factory floor.

3. Somber Tour
Glengarry captain Don Madsen and his family view the Bayport facility by boat during the 1965 flood.

4. Andersen House Threatened
In 1965, rising water engulfed the Andersen House in Bayport, but there was no permanent damage.

36

3

4

37

community

1

2

3 →

Philanthropy

From the company's earliest years, charitable giving has been a rich and pervasive part of Andersen's culture — a value ranking high along with the company's dedication to products, people, and business growth. At first philanthropy was done informally by members of the Andersen family. Stories abound of struggling Andersen workers receiving advances on their paycheck and of widows receiving unsolicited cash gifts from the company. Company records show decisions to pay off mortgages for the survivors of deceased employees, to hire in-home nursing for ill workers, and to financially support employees and their children who were having a hard time paying for college. During the Great Depression, Fred Andersen kept chickens and dairy cows to provide food for the Bayport community, and later his foster-son Hugh Andersen assisted people who needed funds for chemical dependency treatment.

The company's legacy of formal philanthropy started in 1941 with the creation of the Bayport Foundation, whose purpose was to assist needy people, improve living conditions, and support education and scientific research. It was named after the company's hometown, rather than after the company, in keeping with Andersen's wish not to call attention to its charitable giving, and it was an early advocate of assisting the community without regard to age, sex, race, or religion. "An important Andersen family philosophy is embodied in the foundation,"

says company board chair Sarah Andersen, who is Fred Andersen's granddaughter. "We give back to the community because the employees have greatly contributed to the success of the company."

Although the Bayport Foundation now receives regular support from the Andersen Corporation, Andersen family funds began it. The foundation donated $1,012 in 1941 and recent annual contributions have reached $2.3 million. "The foundation's board understood the meaning of 'wellness' well ahead of most other people," says Pat Riley, senior vice president of operations and president of the foundation. "Preventive medical care was an important investment in the community, and our funding shows that. One of the first major gifts was a $10,000 donation to the University of Minnesota in 1947 for cancer research." Today the foundation contributes to such community partners as the Red Cross, the United Negro College Fund, Courage Center, Boy Scouts of America, Twin Cities Public Television, and the Hudson Hospital in Hudson, Wis., which recently renovated its facility and opened a healing garden with foundation support.

For decades, the company's top executives directed the course of Andersen's giving according to their own perceptions of the community's need. The company almost always made its donations anonymously. In the 1990s, though, Andersen Corporation turned its attention to articulating its purpose and strategy for giving. The company's

38

1. True Giving
Projects such as this Andersen blood drive are important signs of employees' commitment to their communities.

2-3. Affordable Housing
Since 1995, Andersen and its employees have joined forces with Habitat for Humanity to build affordable housing across North America.

39

low philanthropic profile "seemed ironic considering our commitment to supporting the community," says Jay Lund, senior vice president of sales and logistics. "Don Garofalo was the first to recognize that it was a core value of our company to be better organized and ultimately more visible in our community." The result was the company's first formal philanthropic plan in 1999, which focuses on creating affordable housing, promoting progress in the practice of architecture and design, encouraging advancement in the building industry, and improving the welfare of people in Andersen's communities across North America. "Profitability is important, but you need a broader view of the world in order to achieve true success," says Jay Lund.

As a result, Andersen has revitalized its role as a community partner. Some of its recent philanthropic projects include:

— The sponsorship of an exhibition of work by architect Frank Lloyd Wright at the Museum of Modern Art in New York.

— A five-year collaboration with Walker Art Center in Minneapolis to feature in-depth looks at individual works of art, movements, or artistic practices, in the museum's Andersen Window Gallery, which was built in part from Fibrex material.

— A long-term relationship with the University of Minnesota, funding a scholarship for students pursuing a degree in the area of Forest Products, which serves to advance the building industry.

— Contributing to the Minnesota Environmental Initiative, which brings together representatives from environmental groups, businesses, communities, and governmental agencies to address environmental issues in our communities.

With a donation of $300,000 worth of windows in 1995, Andersen Corporation began a fruitful partnership with Habitat for Humanity, which uses volunteer labor and donated building materials to raise affordable housing across the United States. The collaboration has grown mightily since then, with Andersen and its five related foundations beginning an initiative in 2003 to contribute $5 million for the construction of 100 homes in North America over the next five years. The organization's mission to eliminate poverty housing and homelessness throughout the world is a great match for Andersen's focus on helping to create beautiful, functional, and energy-efficient homes. Andersen hosted the first-ever CEO Build with Habitat in 2001, which built two homes with business-leader volunteers and is now an annual event; provided 60 women volunteers to lead the construction of two homes as part of the "Women Build" project of Twin Cities Habitat for Humanity; and participated in the building of Habitat's 100,000th home. So far, Andersen employees have given nearly 20,000 volunteer hours to Habitat.

"This is the kind of volunteer work that Andersen people love to do, using their hard labor to build something that rises right before their eyes,"

40

1. Andersen Window Gallery
For several years, Andersen
partnered with Walker Art Center
in Minneapolis to present
exhibitions of contemporary art
in the museum's Andersen
Window Gallery.

says Susan Roeder, Andersen's Community Relations manager. Andersen employees, she added, devote volunteer hours to many other community organizations and projects, including Junior Achievement, Red Cross Blood Drive, Multiple Sclerosis Society's MS 150 Bike Race, and the Holiday Gift Drive.

In the 1950s, Andersen began its highly successful alliance with the United Way. The annual fundraising effort now raises more than $1 million for area United Way chapters, with employees contributing half the total. In the past five years, Andersen and its employees have raised $3 million through the campaign, which helps the United Way provide food and shelter, increased employment, and improved health to nearly one in four people in Andersen's communities.

"We have worked to raise the visibility of Andersen as an outstanding corporate citizen through community involvement, corporate and foundation giving, and strategic media relations," says Maureen McDonough, director of Corporate Communications. "It is good for the company in many ways: it helps to shape perceptions, build brand loyalty, and ultimately, impact the bottom line."

The effect on the world outside Andersen is undeniable. "I attribute a great portion of our hospital's success to the consistent participation and support of the Andersen family and the foundations in this community," says Jeff Robertson, CEO of Lakeview Hospital in Stillwater, Minn., the beneficiary of more than $10 million in Andersen philanthropy during the past decade.

Andersen Family Foundations

Over the past decades, several foundations have been established to manage the charitable giving of Andersen family members. Each has a unique mission.

In 1922 Fred Andersen gave $2,000 for the construction of Lakeshore Park in Hudson, Wisc., a gift in memory of his late brother Herbert. The Andersen family has continued to give to the community through several family foundations that began donating money to worthy causes in the late 1950s. In 1959, Fred and Kitty Andersen created the Andersen Foundation in order to support causes that closely reflected their personal interests and beliefs. Fred was most interested in funding higher education, and Kitty cared most about young people, the elderly, and those with special needs. The Andersen Foundation is now one of the ten largest grantmakers in Minnesota with annual gifts of more than $22 million. The recent donor of $2 million to the Hudson Memorial Health Foundation, it supports educational institutions and nonprofit organizations that provide youth, elderly and health services in the St. Croix Valley.

Kitty Andersen's personal legacy, the Katherine B. Andersen Fund of the Saint Paul Foundation, supports the kinds of projects that Kitty funded during her life, including youth and elderly programs. "Kitty taught me to put time and effort into an organization and never to just put my name on the board roster," observes Sarah Andersen.

Hugh J. Andersen took to heart the values taught by Fred C. Andersen about responsibility to community. Resolved to share his resources with others in need, he created the Hugh J. Andersen Foundation in 1962 with a mission to give back to the community through focused efforts that foster inclusivity, promote equality and lead to increased human independence, self-sufficiency and dignity. It continues today as a family foundation with a commitment to building and strengthening healthy communities. The foundation is currently directed by Hugh's daughters, Christine Andersen and Sarah Andersen, as well as Bill Rubenstein, their late sister Carol's husband. "Our parents were gone before they had a chance to teach us about foundation giving," says Sarah. "My sisters and I had to learn on the job. The gift our father gave us was the strong belief that we should give the way we wanted to give and not be encumbered by the past. The foundation gave us a very special opportunity to grow closer and talk about things that were important to us." Today, they see themselves as grant makers, innovators, educators, partners and convenors. "We continue to change and to respond with our hearts, but we also have organization and structure that ensures we are fair and careful in our giving," Sarah notes.

The family of Betty and Bill Hulings has launched its own foundations within the HRK Foundation, which seeks to promote healthy families and communities, improve the quality of and access to education, and strengthen the fabric of our society. These foundations frequently support housing, health, human services, and the arts.

While the family foundations now have individual geographic and focus areas for their giving, they all continue to believe deeply in giving back to the community in the form of time, talent, and treasure. They occasionally combine efforts. "In the late 1980s the family foundations worked together to build a new library for the city of Bayport," says Sarah Andersen. "The library board had asked for some money to add a room for a few computers. We asked them to consider what they would need for the next 25 years in a library. A whole new location with much greater library space and community meeting space was created instead." The family's Next Generation Fund is designed to help the youngest members of the Andersen family learn about their philanthropic legacy and discover how to make their own philanthropic decisions.

43

Safeguarding the Environment

Natural resources have always been important to Andersen Corporation, and the company has worked to safeguard those resources for its communities and its business. Andersen, after all, is in the business of helping build and enhance homes, and the environment is everyone's home. Over the decades, the company has learned to approach manufacturing with the aim of preserving and protecting resources. In its own facilities, Andersen takes pride in the extent to which it reduces consumption, reuses materials, reclaims resources, and recycles.

Since **1988**, for instance, the solid waste bound for the landfill from Andersen's plant in Bayport has been reduced by 97 percent. During the same time, the plant's toxic emissions have declined 98 percent. Twice in the **1990s** Green Seal, an environmental labeling advocacy organization, recognized Andersen for the energy efficiency of its products. In **1998** the U.S. Environmental Protection Agency named the company the outstanding Energy Star Homes Manufacturer Ally, making Andersen the first window and patio door manufacturer to receive this honor.

Andersen began the new millennium with a widely applauded public commitment not to source wood from endangered forests and to instead give preference to wood supplied by producers who follow responsible forestry management practices.

New materials, as well as new manufacturing practices, contribute to these environmental

distinctions. Fibrex material, the composite building compound that Andersen developed during the **1990s**, blends synthetics with reclaimed wood fiber that comes directly from the company's manufacturing processes. In the future, the increased use of Fibrex material in Andersen products will reduce its need for lumber and further reduce volatile emissions.

Back in **1924**, company president Fred Andersen hired a crew to plant one thousand northern white pine seedlings on the Point, a spit of land he owned near the Bayport plant. He also helped create public parks and camping areas throughout the region. His appreciation for natural beauty persists in the environmental vision of Andersen Corporation today.

1-2. A Commitment to the Environment
Throughout its history, Andersen has had the goal of preserving and protecting resources.

44

Philanthropy

"FROM THOSE TO WHOM MUCH HAS BEEN GIVEN, MUCH SHALL BE REQUIRED"

—Philanthropic philosophy of Betty and Bill Hulings

48

49

50

51

Family

The one thing many people know about Andersen Corporation founder Hans Andersen is that his first words of English were "All together, boys!", the rallying cry he constantly heard from his fellow lumberjacks early in his life. As the story goes, Hans enjoyed the comic effect of repeating the phrase when passing food to his dining companions. — While the tale may not be true, it has served for many decades as a succinct summation of Hans' philosophy of regarding everyone in his business as equal partners with common interests. The leaders that followed him in the Andersen Corporation adopted this philosophy as well. — If any one thing is most distinctive about Andersen's history, it is how the deep relationships between Andersen people have contributed to the company's success. Like members of a **family**, employees struggle together, brainstorm together, play together, and work hard together. And the rewards have spread throughout the workforce.

All in the Family

In the turn-of-the-century household of Hans and Sadie Andersen in Hudson, Wisconsin, the dining table was a place of discussion and speculation. Hans, the owner of a successful lumberyard in town, had many times told his sons Herbert and Fred that they could pursue any profession they wanted and that he would find any necessary funds for their education. As the water quietly lapped against the east bank of the St. Croix River a few blocks away, Hans, Sadie, Herbert, Fred, and their sister Mary (Molly), when she visited from college, repeatedly talked over what might come in the future.

The future arrived in **1903**. Herbert and Fred, 18 and 16 years old respectively, knew they didn't want to attend law school, medical school, or anything like that. They wanted to learn a business. They wanted to work with their father. On the day after they both graduated from Hudson High School, June 3, **1903**, the boys joined the small workforce of Hans' lumberyard.

Several weeks later, on July 25, **1903**, the family again gathered around the dining table for an especially important event — the signing of the articles of incorporation of the Andersen Lumber Company, the business that would grow into the Andersen Corporation. The incorporation papers laid out a range of activities that the company could pursue, including the selling of lumber, the operation of planing mills, the purchase and sale of real estate and buildings, and, most importantly, "the manufacture of logs and lumber into building materials." With a

capital investment of $10,000, the family wanted to set off in a new direction: the manufacture of window frames in a factory building in Hudson.

Herbert and Fred were still too young to participate as legal partners (Hans, Sadie, and the family attorney were the initial legal owners), but they were already full partners in spirit. Soon Herbert would leave home to apprentice at the Weyerhaeuser lumber mill at Lake Nebagamon, Wisconsin. Fred would focus his energies on managing the family's new lumberyard in Afton, Minnesota. After a year, the brothers returned to work in Hudson to devote their time to the window frame business. Their brainpower, backs, and newly gained experience were needed.

The family company began making window frames in mid-**1904**. Herbert took charge of the work crew, which soon grew to a dozen men. Fred helped with sales. Conditions in the plant were harsh because the building was poorly heated. But after a year, the factory was breaking even — making 120 frames a day — and on the verge of strong growth. The family decided to invest in a small addition to the factory. By **1909**, the Andersen Lumber Company was producing more than 100,000 frames per year.

Within a few years, as production further increased, Hans and his family agreed that the company needed a new and substantially larger plant. They bought a site across the river in South Stillwater (later renamed Bayport), and in **1912** they began building a new Andersen Lumber Company factory, the first manufacturing facility in the city. Hans and

3

4

Herbert together supervised the construction. They arranged for the relocation of most of the equipment by horse-drawn sled across the river ice, but the heaviest machines had to travel a circuitous path by rail. The *Hudson Star-Observer* lamented the loss, but admitted that "a removal to less crowded quarters was an absolute necessity which perhaps has been long delayed more from a sentimental regard for Hudson and its people than for any good business reason."

The new facility had 66,362 square feet, a many-fold increase over the space available in Hudson. The plant went into full production on March 17, **1913**. William "Dougie" Goulette, who began his 50-year-long Andersen career on the day the plant opened, recalled that the company's first products made in South Stillwater were window and door frames, wood moulding, and a few kinds of hardwood flooring. The company's output of window frames reached a new record of 143,000 the first year in Minnesota.

55

1. Father and Sons
Hans Andersen drives a wagon with passengers Fred and Herbert, circa 1903.

2. Andersen House in Hudson
The home of Hans and Sadie Andersen and their family, photographed on May 9, 1903.

3. Andersen Factory, circa 1914
Marcus Solheim, inventor of a dado machine and other ingeniously designed equipment that Andersen used for years

in frame production, stands at the right. He remained an active employee past the age of 80.

4. Andersen Incorporation Papers
Members of the Andersen family and their attorney signed the articles of incorporation in July 1903. The company celebrated the centennial of that event, Founders Day, on July 19, 2003.

1

2

The Women of Andersen

Although the leadership ranks of Andersen through the 1970s might have looked like a men's club, with women absent from the most important roles, several women made contributions to the company at crucial periods in its history. Sadie Andersen, Hans Andersen's second wife, was a founding partner in the Andersen Lumber Company in 1903, and her ideas helped direct the launch of the fledgling enterprise.

In much the same way, Mary "Molly" Andersen, Fred and Herbert's sister, provided energy and creative thoughts to the new business. A graduate of the University of Wisconsin-Madison with a mind as nimble as her brothers', Mary established the first American Field Service recreation camp for U.S. military nurses in Europe during World War I. She lived until 1947 and saw Andersen Corporation grow into a large, successful business.

Two other women helped behind the scenes to lead the company during Andersen's first 75 years. Kitty Andersen, Fred's second wife, played a crucial role in helping Andersen adjust to wartime conditions by directing the addition of women to the factory workforce during World War II. She served on the board of directors for a half-century, guiding the company through years of remarkable growth. Kitty died in 1996. Betty Andersen Hulings, Fred's niece who became his foster daughter, and wife of company president Bill Hulings, was a strong

presence who frequently represented the company at trade shows and other events and spent 60 years on the board of directors.

The company's management felt reluctant to accept contributions from Andersen women of the generation that followed. "We were five women who were never groomed to be a part of the business," says Christine Andersen, daughter of Hugh, Fred's nephew whom he raised as his own son. "The one way for members of the family to start in the company was by unloading boxcars, and everyone thought women couldn't do that." Mary Hulings Rice and Martha Hulings Kaemmer, daughters of Betty and Bill Hulings, recall that — as many other girls of that era were treated — they were not even allowed inside the Andersen plant until they were 16.

The tide turned in 1983, when Sarah Andersen, another of Hugh's daughters, was elected to the board of directors. She worked to strengthen the governing responsibilities of the board and in 1993 became its chair.

1. Sadie Andersen
Sarah "Sadie" McDonald Andersen was a founder of the Andersen Lumber Company.

2. Molly Andersen
Mary "Molly" Andersen, Fred and Herbert Andersen's sister, took part in the creation of the company and lived long enough to see its enormous success.

3. Hans with His Children
Hans poses with (left to right) Fred, Herbert, and Molly in a portrait taken about 1892.

family

Hans Andersen

Hans Andersen, the founder of the Andersen Corporation, stood about six feet tall. He usually wore long sideburns and a large bushy mustache, although the best surviving photo shows him clean-shaven. His most striking features, however, were his eyes — intelligent and clear eyes that stare out of the frame of the picture and into a future that not only seems to please him, but appears to be exactly what he expected to see.

People called him a perfectionist (he ran his businesses and his personal finances according to strict budgets), generous (he shared his company's profits with employees when nobody expected him to), unpretentious (when workers were installing the boiler for the new South Stillwater plant, he got down on his knees with a trowel and pitched in, even though he was wearing a business suit), and, despite his Danish birth and childhood, an assimilated American (he spoke English without an accent).

But more important than any of that, at least as far as the success of the Andersen Corporation is concerned, was his extraordinary skill as an entrepreneur and businessman. First, Hans recognized that the building industry needed high-quality factory-produced window frames to replace the handmade frames that builders laboriously, and sometimes inaccurately, put together at construction sites. He formed the Andersen Lumber Company to meet that need. Then, in 1905, Hans revolutionized the American building materials industry by inventing the "two-bundle" method of packaging unassembled window frames. He designed eleven sets of horizontal parts in different lengths and another eleven sets of vertical parts in different lengths, enabling his company to provide window frames in 121 sizes that fit together in less than ten minutes, without additional trimming. In addition, all of the window sizes could be assembled from parts economically shipped and stored in just two bundles. This concept, which greatly benefited wholesalers and builders, launched the company on its early national success.

Finally, Hans was one of the first American business owners to realize that treating employees as an equal partner was more than humane — it was good for business. His introduction of a profit sharing system built loyalty, improved the quality of work, and produced a stable workforce.

After 1896, Hans made Hudson his permanent home. He was in Hudson on December 24, 1914, when — after signing the first batch of profit sharing checks in his company's history — he collapsed in the street and died from a heart attack at the age of 60.

The community plunged into mourning. The Andersen plant closed and nearly the entire workforce took a special train to Hudson for the funeral. Herbert and Fred Andersen, still young men, were left in charge of the business. Could the Andersen Lumber Company continue its run of success?

58

60

1. Hans Andersen
A portrait from around 1880.

2. Naturalization Documents
The legal papers that officially
recognized Hans Andersen's
U.S. citizenship.

Fred Andersen

He listened and let others argue. Sometimes he rocked in his swivel chair or drew on his cigarette and let the ashes dance across the surface of his necktie. Then, "without raising his voice, but by sheer logic, he would calm things down and put everything into perspective," recalled an associate who often observed Fred Andersen in meetings, "like the calmness that follows lightning and thunder."

Fred Cummings Andersen — the man who became the president of his family's company at the age of 28, guided the business through world wars and revolutions in manufacturing and marketing, and displayed a rare ability to place his faith in the right person at the right time — was a strong presence at the Andersen Corporation for more than 75 years. For many, he personified the company, and for others he symbolized its interest in the welfare of its employees. A quarter-century after his death, his mark still endures.

Fred, born in **1886** in Spring Valley, Minnesota, lost his mother when he was four. Reared by his father, lumberyard and wood mill owner Hans Andersen, and his stepmother Sadie Andersen, he moved frequently with his family until the Andersens settled in Hudson, Wisconsin, in **1896**. As a high school student he declared his ambition to learn the lumber business from his father, and he teamed up with his father, stepmother, brother and sister to form the Andersen Lumber Company in **1903**.

Fred gained his first true taste of the business as the manager of the Andersen lumberyard in Afton, Minnesota. He tried some interesting ways of building new business. "I remember he was after my dad to teach him to play the violin and to teach him some German," said Ben Richert, who met Fred in Afton. "There were a lot of German-speaking people in the area, and Fred felt it would help him communicate better with his customers."

In **1905**, Fred began selling his company's new "two-bundle" window frames to wholesalers in the Twin Cities. He had no car or carriage. The disassembled frames made "exceedingly awkward packages to carry around on street cars," he later remembered. "I guess the people thought I was crazy, but I covered St. Paul and Minneapolis and succeeded in introducing the goods in a small way." Two dealers alone were responsible for purchases of 10,000 frames.

Soon after, he became a director and vice president of the company. Though his astigmatism prevented him from becoming a great mechanic or designer, and he lacked a college education, his talents soon rose to the surface: he was a loquacious and effective salesman; he could quickly judge the potential of other people; and he had faith in his own decisions. With his father he shared a desire to get to

62

63

family

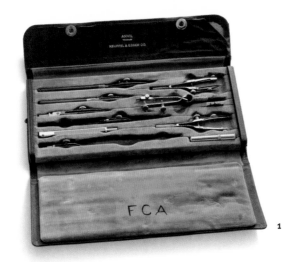

know his employees, whom he regarded as his allies. "Here at Andersen," he wrote at the end of his career, "we have a tradition of sharing problems and success in a true spirit of cooperation, wherein interests of owners and workers are similar. What benefits one, benefits all. Everyone is part of a genuine working partnership. This has been our guiding philosophy and it has worked."

When Hans died suddenly at the end of **1914**, Fred ascended to the presidency of the company, sharing management responsibilities with his brother Herbert, the vice president and secretary-treasurer. Among his earliest major decisions was the company's branching off into the retail lumberyard business in **1915**. He later presided over the company's introduction of the Master Frame and the first fully assembled windows, the arduous years of the Great Depression, the conversion to war production during World War II, and the decision to experiment with plastics as a protective sheath for windows.

As much as for these accomplishments, though, Fred is remembered for his one-of-a-kind personality. He loved things red — flowers, furniture, neck ties. A stickler for grammatical accuracy, he once saw a letter from a customer that included the phrase, "He can make them go good," and penciled in the margin, "An adjective used as an adverb — am I right?" His house practically sat on company property, drawing heat and electricity from the main plant. He often fled Bayport for the quiet and natural beauty of Sand Island in Lake Superior, only to use

that time to work on window designs. In a company of teasers and jokers, his pranks were memorable. He sometimes brought his dog Spunk to executive meetings, referring to the mutt as "one of the vice presidents" and halting the proceedings to let the canine VP outdoors. At the party for president Earl Swanson's 40-year anniversary with the company, he leaned over toward Earl and said, "You know, Earl, I checked up the other day, and you've never been taken off the list of temporary employees, so you better watch your step."

He was an old-style chief executive who radiated power and exercised it with restraint. "If you did something he didn't like, you knew it," says his granddaughter Mary Hulings Rice. "It was never a screaming, yelling thing. It was very quiet and commanding."

When he died in **1979** at the age of 92, a part of the Andersen Corporation's history passed on with him. Eulogies praised his concern for the community, his generosity to countless charities, his inventions and innovations. The *Frame Maker* gave him the simplest and truest memorial: "He was the guiding force in the growth of Andersen Corporation."

2

3

4

5

1. Drafting Tools
Fred Andersen took part in the design of many Andersen products, as his patents and these tools testify.

2. Fred Andersen at His Desk
For his entire career, Fred maintained an "open door" policy, welcoming all employees and visitors to his office at nearly any time.

3. Three-Quarters of a Century
Fred Andersen remained an Andersen employee for more than 75 years, longer than anyone else in company history.

4. Fred Andersen with Employees, Circa 1950
Fred is still known for his ability to remember the names of virtually every Andersen employee who worked during his presidency.

5. Fred with Spunk
Fred and Kitty Andersen were both fond of dogs, and he's shown here with Spunk, the pooch he named an honorary vice president.

Herbert Andersen

Herbert Andersen, Fred's older brother and a partner in the company for 18 years, remains an elusive figure, someone largely lost to history. He apparently spoke little, although he loved to sing. He had a mild face and a concerned gaze. Mechanically gifted, he supervised the operation of the plant after Hans' death, while Fred looked after purchasing, planning, sales, and administration.

Herbert's daughter, Betty Andersen Hulings, called him "the first main machinist and engineer at the factory. I remember him taking me into the factory when I was three or four and showing me this enormous wheel that went down below the floor level. That had something to do with making electricity for us."

Others remembered Herbert as an expert at averting problems. "Herbert often walked through the plant to ask the men if they had any suggestions or beefs, rather than waiting for some problems to develop," said early employee Louis Anderson.

For his wedding portrait in **1913**, Herbert wore a light-colored suit and parted his hair down the middle. His bride, Frances Helms Andersen, died from tuberculosis in **1920**, soon after bearing two children, Betty and Hugh.

Herbert took this loss very hard, and he died less than two years later at the age of 36. "Fred told me one time he felt Herbert died of a broken heart — just lost his will to live," said Earl Swanson. The actual cause of death was tubercular pericarditis, a disease of the heart cavity. Several area businesses closed for Herbert's funeral, and the South Stillwater village council passed a resolution mourning his death.

1

1. Herbert's Notebook
Herbert Andersen's pocket
notebook reflects his attention
to the details of pricing,
shipping, and manufacturing
window frames.

1

2

Andersen Families

If you worked at Andersen's Bayport facility anytime between 1920 and now, you probably knew someone named Speich. Five generations of Speichs have worked at Andersen, beginning with Pete Speich, a painter and immigrant from Switzerland. The Speich family is notable for its long association with Andersen, but many groups of family members, some larger in number than the Speichs, have joined the company's workforce over the years. And Andersen has welcomed them. Started by a family, the company has found that family connections can contribute to the gathering of the steady, hardworking group of partners that Andersen has always been lucky to employ.

Dave Speich, Pete's grandson, retired in 1987 after 37 years at Andersen working in the factory, in the sales department, in the order department, in sales promotion, as service department manager, and finally as quality control manager. He was followed into the Andersen workforce by his three sons — Dan, Tim, and Jon — as well as by his daughter Sally, who worked summers while a student.

"My dad, Wesley Speich, worked 44 years at Andersen, mainly in the cutting room, and he retired as a foreman and lead supervisor," Dave recalls. "I remember going in to visit him at the plant. People would bring in pots of beans to cook slowly around the boilers, and as a kid I would take the beans home. At 16, I was able to start working at Andersen, but not with the heavy machines. I began in

True as a Bell

Some phrases tumble from the mouths of Andersen's Bayport employees with surprising regularity: "My Dad worked here." "My sister works here, too." "All of my kids came to work at Andersen, either permanently or during the summers." "Grandpa was a foreman." "I'm not sure how many of us have worked here — I lost track."

Nine members of the Bell family once worked at the Bayport plant at one time. Canadian in origin, the family has included many colorful characters, not the least of which were brothers Eugene "Peanuts" Bell and Le Roy "Ringer" Bell. Peanuts retired after 39 years of service; Ringer retired with 40 years. (Their brother George also worked 40 years at Andersen.) About a year

before Ringer's death in 2002, the two brothers got together for an animated discussion of their histories with Andersen. Here are excerpts.

Peanuts : I got my nickname when I was a small baby in my buggy. Someone said, "Can I see that little peanut?"

Ringer : My nickname came from my dad, who saw me throwing ringers in a game at the State Fair.

Peanuts : I graduated from Stillwater High School on a Friday in 1942. I started working at Andersen on Monday. My starting pay was 32 cents an hour. I was there almost my whole career, except for four years I spent in the military. It was easy for me to walk to work, the job was fine, and there was just no reason to leave.

1958 by working two days a week, hauling cartons from the Quonset hut near the NSP plant. I'm retired now, but I still keep a copy of the Andersen catalogue in my car."

His son Dan, now a mechanic supervisor at Andersen, remembers his own boyhood visits to see Dave at work. "When I would go fishing, I'd have the fish weighed on a scale in the boiler room. I'd go down there, and I thought I was going some-place really special," he says. "Then I started working as a lifeguard at the Quarter Century Club picnics, and I worked summers in maintenance. It had always been in the back of my mind to work at Andersen, even though I looked at other companies. I got my training in hydraulics, started fulltime with Andersen in **1975**, and went into the garage as a mechanic.

I had to prove my worth more than the rest of the guys because of my family. I took extra classes in order to be a cut above the rest."

With so many Andersen workers in the family, conversations at Speich reunions can sound very mysterious to outsiders. "We talk about windows — we can just rattle off the model numbers," Dan says. "And let me tell you, when Dad installed the Andersen windows in our family cabin, he would not take his sons' advice."

Ringer : I was in the Civilian Conservation Corps during the Great Depression and began working at Andersen in June **1939**. I was piling lum-ber. In the first load I lifted, I spilled two boards. Then, later, I took a job lubricating all the machines in the plant. It took four months to get around to all of them. I eventually figured that if you're going to work in a factory, Andersen is as good as it's going to get.

Peanuts : Neither of us was ever laid off. At times, maybe when business was slow, we were farmed out to different departments. I remember that Fred Andersen's neckties were full of cigarette holes. He wouldn't take his cigarette out of his mouth. I don't care if you had a meeting with God Almighty, you canceled it to meet with Mr. Andersen.

1-4. Family Photos
A gallery of pictures of families who served as Andersen employees: the Hayners (1953), the Bells (circa 1949), the Dahls (1959), and the Browns (1965).

Sharing the Wealth

In the spring of 1917, Fred Andersen wrote a letter to his uncle in Sweden, trying to explain his company's practice of giving away a share of the profits each year to its employees. "Father started [the profit sharing plan] just before he died, and paid each man who had been in our employ a year an amount equal to 5 percent of the compensation received during the past year. It took a certain part of our net profits to do this, and each year we planned on devoting about an equal proportion of our net profits to the same purpose," he wrote. The intention, he said, "was that this would create an old age fund."

In 1914, when the Andersen Lumber Company introduced its profit sharing plan, founder Hans Andersen was drawing a salary of $2,000 per year — adjusted for inflation, about $34,400 in today's dollars. "He didn't wait until he got in the big money before he wanted to have his partners share in the profits," said son Fred Andersen. The tiny number of other American manufacturers then with profit sharing arrangements — Eastman Kodak Company started its plan in 1912 — were much bigger concerns than the small window-frame maker in Bayport.

At a meeting around the dining room table, Hans told his family of his reasons for wanting to share the profits. "Father's idea was that we should pay top wages in the woodworking industry, and then — after taking a reasonable 6 percent of year-end profits for the investors who had created and managed the business — the remaining money should be shared with employees," Fred recalled.

The Great Depression

The Depression years of 1929 through 1938 marked not only an extended spell of unprofitability for Andersen, but also a fight for the company's very survival. In the first six years of the downturn, Andersen's sales withered — building construction was hit especially hard by the sickly economy — and losses of nearly a half-million dollars accumulated. The company responded by trimming the workforce and at one point reducing everyone who remained to a three-day week.

Even so, the company found itself in serious financial trouble, with heavy debts. "I remember going to some of the bank officers in Minneapolis with [Fred].... It was a close call," said Earl Swanson, then Fred Andersen's personal assistant. "They almost shut him down. But he was persuasive and said he could do it and he'd come back. He was a good salesman. It was tough. He had to lay off so many people who didn't have any other work to do. He had to reduce wages several times. I remember going out in the factory with him and he'd stand up on the table and say, 'Here I am again. If we're going to stay in business, we've got to cut wages again.' He did it, but it hurt him more than anything I can remember." At one point, when there were few orders to fill, the company kept employees on the payroll by assigning them to plant a thousand elm tree seedlings purchased from a nursery. Despite it all, in 1934,

3

Hans and his family built a success-sharing philosophy that remains strikingly modern today. Management and employees, they believed, shared responsibility for the health of the company. Given that partnership, the two should also share the rewards.

During the **1980s**, the profit sharing disbursements reached stratospheric levels, even as market share began to decline. These lavish distributions foretold trouble. While employees enjoyed the extra income, the payout produced unrealistic expectations of future income and profits. Customers resented Andersen's high profit sharing. "These were Andersen's darkest days," says CEO Don Garofalo. "The big profit sharing percentages of those years were the result of not reinvesting

4

sufficiently in the business to enable the company to maintain its market share." It took a decisive redirection of Andersen ten years later to set things right.

Although each business unit upholds this longstanding value in different ways, Andersen's commitment to sharing its success with employees remains in place today. This extraordinary record speaks volumes about how much the company appreciates the dedicated efforts of the Andersen workforce.

Fred Andersen confidently predicted that profitability would return. "We want to assure you," he wrote to all employees, "that our well established policy of many years' standing — sharing prosperity with our men — is still the policy of this company."

Andersen got back on track with a profit sharing of 9 percent in **1937**, and two years later returned to a chain of profitability that has not yet been broken.

1. Profit Sharing Celebration
There is always an atmosphere of pride and enthusiasm at the annual Bayport event, shown here in the late 1990s.

2. Hearing Good News
Andersen employees and their families sat on barrels and improvised benches at a profit sharing announcement of the 1950s.

3. On the Stage
Employees enjoyed a mix of speakers, music, and raffles at the profit sharing celebrations of the mid-20th century.

4. The Letter
For 45 years, Andersen employees received news of their profit sharing benefits in letters from Fred Andersen. The letters shown here, received by Harry Groth, date from 1925 and 1956.

family

1

2

Beyond the Paycheck

"There is a richness at Andersen in its human resources tradition," says Mary Carter, the company's senior vice president of human resources and communications. "Hans Andersen was not only a leader in manufacturing, but also in human resources. We sometimes think that kind of tradition exists everywhere, but it isn't so. There's been an unusually consistent commitment here to be a good employer."

Hans' deep regard for employees spread throughout the company. "He was really an early leader in the management of human resources," Carter says. "He truly understood how to motivate people. He knew that in order to hire the best people, you have to pay top wages. It was important for him to provide steady employment as much as possible, and he preferred to reward employees based on the performance of the company. These are all core principles of Andersen Corporation today."

In 1916 the company organized the ALCO Benefit Club, and it served for decades as a mutual benefit pool funded by employees and the company to keep wages flowing in the event of long-term illnesses or injuries. (ALCO was short for Andersen Lumber Company; the organization survives today as a social club.) It also assisted with medical treatment costs long before employees commonly received health insurance.

The company introduced many other benefits at early dates:
— Company-paid group life insurance arrived in 1919.
— Paid vacations were first offered in 1923.
— Beginning in 1931, a liberal Income Security Plan designed for the lean years of the Great Depression allowed employees to draw advances on their salaries.
— Hospitalization insurance was offered in 1938.
— A company-funded pension plan began in 1943.
— Andersen established an employee stock ownership plan in 1975, and it remains an important part of what binds Andersen to its employees. A continuation of Hans Andersen's desire to share the company's successes with employees, the decision to give shares of Andersen stock to large numbers of eligible workers every year is part of the company's strategy to offer employees many ways to build their funds for retirement, encourage people to remain with Andersen, and to keep the ownership of the company in the hands of those who have worked the hardest for it and care the most about it.

In some ways, Andersen is a much different business to work for than it was even a few years

3

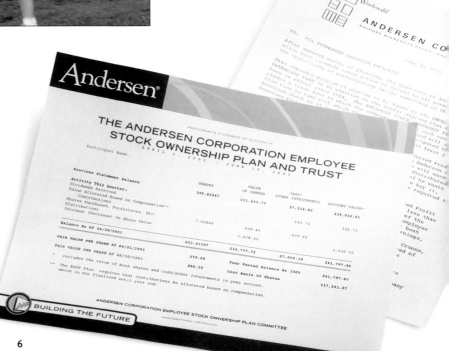

6

73

ago. In the past decade, the company's work force has tripled in size. Bayport is no longer the only place where employees work, and within the company you can hear as many as nine different languages. Manufacturing workers used to make up the majority of the work force, but now most Andersen employees work in office, service, or technological capacities. Providing employees with needed information and encouraging them to develop their own leadership abilities have become top company priorities. In the future, Andersen employees will be more dispersed than ever throughout North America, and they will be closer to customers.

These changes have not eroded Andersen's commitment to its people. More than ever, the company is concerned for its employees' well-being, gives them opportunities for growth and long-term employment, offers workers a progressive sharing of rewards, communicates its strategies, recognizes and rewards good performance, and tries to do what's right as an employer. Thank you, Hans Andersen, for the great example you've left.

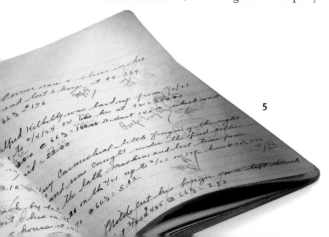

5

1-4. Picnic Fun
A button and images from the annual ALCO picnic, in which Andersen employees come together to celebrate the summer.

5. Injury Record
A logbook recorded injuries that Andersen employees sustained on the job through much of the 1920s. Long concerned about these injuries, the company introduced long-term disability benefits in 1916.

6. Stock Plan Papers
For decades, the Employee Stock Ownership Plan has allowed many employees to more directly benefit from the company's success.

family

Earl Swanson

In **1927** a new Andersen employee, a 16-year-old named Earl Swanson, sat at his drafting table. A tall bespectacled man approached him and asked to borrow a measuring tape. Earl was surprised to find out that he was speaking with Fred Andersen, the president of the company.

Thus began an unusual relationship that greatly enriched the lives of each man and guaranteed the Andersen Corporation's future. Earl became Fred's personal secretary.

In **1928** Earl joined Fred in Glendora, California, where Fred was temporarily living because of the poor health of his first wife, Isabel. Together Earl and Fred brainstormed and sketched the initial designs for the Andersen Master Frame window, which offered a break-through in drainage and water protection. On later trips together they kept probing the company's weaknesses and opportunities.

Their bond went beyond professional interests. "He was a second father to me. That's what it really amounted to," Earl said. "After his first wife died, I lived at his house for some months to give him a little company and to work with him. We got along well."

At the age of 26, Earl ascended to plant manager when longtime manager Bud Bird died suddenly. Earl's secretary, Vi Dahl, remembered, "It was fantastic how smoothly Earl took over the reins.

Nothing ever flustered Earl." With nine patents in his name, he acquired the nickname "Pat Pending." He designed the Andersen Horizontal Gliding Window, the first window of its kind.

Over the next 30 years, Earl rose to vice president of manufacturing, president, chairman of the executive committee, and chairman of the board of Andersen Corporation. He was the main force behind the company's expansion into vinyl-clad products, and he hired John Kohl to direct the effort. "Earl was an impressive man. You looked at him and thought, 'He must be the head of the company,' which of course he was," recalls former president Jerry Wulf.

Not long before his death, he met a new employee who commented, "You must be one of the old-timers." Earl nodded. The man continued, "When did you come to Andersen?" "Years ago," Earl replied. "What did you do?" the man asked. Earl answered, "I was in charge of bending paperclips."

When he died in **1999** at the age of 88, he left a high standard of leadership and a lasting legacy for the company — as well as a great many paper clips, beautifully bent.

74

1

Kitty and the Octoberettes

At noon on June 24, 1941, in the sanctuary of St. Mark's Methodist Episcopal Church in Brooklyn, New York, Katherine Dyer Blount married Fred Andersen. She would ever after be known as Kitty Andersen. "We cordially welcome Mrs. Andersen to her new home in Bayport," the *Frame Maker* noted. Bayport — and the Andersen Corporation — had no idea what it was receiving.

Kitty, 36 years old when they married, was a Brooklyn native who had met Fred at Sand Island in Lake Superior, where he owned a group of cabins. She was there visiting an old college roommate. The friends decided to drop in on their widower neighbor to bum cigarettes. Fred opened the door to two cheeky women dressed in Indian costumes. He gave them cigarettes. The one who had her Master's Degree in Science from New York University and who was working on her Ph.D. captured his attention.

The courtship of Fred and Kitty startled many people. One evening they ended a date parked in Fred's car. A police officer, noticing the telltale fogging of the windows, decided to roust the kids inside. His thoughts on discovering the middle-aged occupants can only be guessed. Later, when Fred proposed to her in New York City, Kitty arched her eyebrows and asked to see a ring as evidence of his good faith. Fred got up off his knees, went directly to Tiffany's, and came back with a ring.

Until their marriage, Fred had led a busy, accomplished, but mostly grim life. He had seen his father, mother, brother, sister-in-law, and first wife die under sudden or tragic circumstances. He had taken responsibility for rearing his brother's children. He had watched his business stall and plummet during the Great Depression, coming within an inch of bankruptcy. And as World War II darkened the horizon, he was about to face the temporary disappearance of all his products and customers, to be replaced by government defense work that required the retooling of his plant.

Kitty changed Fred's life, giving him his intellectual match in a partner who teased him, cajoled him, and brought warmth to his existence. She was a tough woman with a big heart and a love of children and animals. (Later, when she had a seat on the Andersen Corporation board of directors, she once arrived late to a meeting, dripping wet. She explained that she had just rescued her dog Baron, who had fallen through the ice on the St. Croix River.)

She found a perfect outlet for her talents a year after her arrival, when the growing numbers of Andersen workers joining the armed forces encouraged the company to begin hiring women in the factory for the first time. The first four female employees in the plant — Nora Kresenke, Erna Munkelwitz, Gretchen Wolff Gibson, and Freda Remseth — began working in October 1942. Many more joined them later that month, and the group became known as the "Octoberettes."

76

The arrival of the Octoberettes brought confusion to the Andersen operation. Some facilities for women, including bathrooms, were lacking. The foremen had no experience as supervisors of women, and some didn't know what to expect from the new employees. When a group of supervisors met in Fred Andersen's home to discuss the problems, Kitty suggested that the company hire a personnel director specifically for the women. Kitty didn't seek the job, but she got it.

Kitty proved to be a worker bee. She interviewed the women applicants, listened sympathetically to their complaints, and acted upon their requests. She made life in the factory more pleasant by persuading the men in charge to pipe in music and install an effective forced-air heating system to replace the old steam heating. She arranged for the availability of hot lunches for workers. If she suspected the lifting on the job was too heavy for the women, she would try it herself. "Mrs. Andersen was lovely to all of us," Freda Remseth remembered. "She looked out for all the girls, and frequently came into the factory to check on working conditions — she was exactly what we needed to get everything working smoothly."

Nine of the first fourteen Octoberettes were still Andersen employees after a year. For a time, a third of the employees who received Suggestion Plan cash awards were women. Remseth, who initially arrived just to help temporarily and began working on a conveyor in the cutting department, enjoyed a 33-year-long career at Andersen.

Andersen's factory doors were now permanently open to women. Two decades later, Viola Gelford became one of the first women traffic managers at any American manufacturing company. Another two decades later, Sarah Andersen became the corporation's first female board chair.

Kitty herself joined the board of directors in 1943 and served for 50 years. An energetic philanthropist and organizer, she devoted much of her time and energy to a variety of community projects and endeavors: blood drives, the Boy and Girl Scouts, activities for senior citizens, support for the Bayport Public Library, and foundation work. After she died in 1996 at the age of 91, the family established the Katherine B. Andersen Youth Science Center, and a fireworks display on her birthday aptly symbolized her effect on the community she adopted.

1. Kitty Andersen
Katherine Blount Andersen energized Andersen Corporation with her ideas, big heart, and generosity.

2. Andersen Generations
Kitty Andersen (center) is flanked by her granddaughter and board chair Sarah Andersen and Sarah's husband Chris Hayner.

3. The Octoberettes
These were nineteen of the women hired on as the first females to work in the Andersen plant in October 1942.

78

79

1. A New Era
During World War II the Andersen plant changed dramatically with the introduction of women production employees.

2. Many Stayed
Erna Munkelwitz (foreground), shown here in 1954, was one of several Octoberettes who remained with Andersen for decades after the end of World War II.

3. Lunch Cart
Kitty Andersen (right) organized a portable hot meal service for the first time in the Andersen plant.

1

Stories from the Plant

The amount of time that people in the Andersen workforce have collectively spent on the job over the course of a century is almost too great to comprehend. Here are some memorable stories from the early years.

Thin Soup, Thin Slices

During World War II, Eleanor Lemke began a service of selling sandwiches and soup in the Andersen plant. Bill Westphal got a bowl of soup one day, and said, "Eleanor, you've got to get a finer screen. There was a piece of meat in my soup."

When the war ended, Avery Hokanson won a contract to operate a cafeteria on the premises. He quickly earned the nickname "Thin Slice." "The nickname was just for laughs," remembered Steve Ridgway, formerly of the order desk. "Hoke served some pretty good meals."

Ross Dahlin, who leads Andersen's international division, agrees. "In 1952 the pork chops were damn good in the cafeteria — also the sauerkraut and stewed potroast," he says. "Hoke kept the same look in the cafeteria from after the war to the 1960s. Sometimes almost everyone in the company was eating in there at once."

Cats in the Sawdust

In the early years, the Andersen factory was full of cats. Especially numerous in the cutting department, they disappeared with the arrival of motorized loading equipment. "I loved to watch the cats," recalled Betty Andersen Hulings, Fred Andersen's foster-daughter who frequently visited the factory as a child. "You couldn't pet the cats. They were too wild."

Andersen Pranks

"There were a lot of hijinks that went on in the factory in the old days," says Allan DeFore. "Some guys used to smear pitch or grease on the handles of tools. Or they'd go to the time clock and move around the cards of the guys they knew were rushing out to get a seat on the bus. Another joke was to place a plank under a load so that the guy couldn't get his jack under it. Sometimes they would load up the adjacent aisles so the loader would have to move them in order to get the plank out, especially if they knew he wanted to duck out five minutes early."

Crossing the Ice

For those commuting to Bayport from Wisconsin, the wintertime choice is bridge or ice. Using the mile-long road over the ice from North Hudson to Bayport Marina can lop up to 20 minutes off the trip. Hundreds choose the ice on some days. Occasionally the trip is not smooth.

2

3

"When I was a young guy, I lived on the north end of Hudson," says George "Gus" Nelson. "One day I really didn't want to be late for work, and I thought if I went across the ice, I'd make it. I got onto the Wisconsin side of the river, and the ice was starting to melt. I was zipping along at 50 to 60 miles per hour. When I got to the Minnesota side I saw there was fifteen feet of open water, so I thought I just had to gun it. Well, cars don't skip like rocks, so I ended up climbing onto the hood."

Longtime Andersen employee Noble Roland found another way to cross the frozen river. "One time when I was skating across to Bayport, I skated into an open spot where the fellows had cut a hole so they could put in a net to catch some fish," he remembered. "But I crawled out in a hurry."

The Bad Old Days

The original factory in Hudson didn't have an outhouse. But a wooden platform led from the shop to the river, and under that was a pile of lumber situated over the St. Croix River that served as an emergency privy. "You could look down and see carp swimming around," Noble Roland said. "One day Fred Andersen came along while I was sitting across a two-by-four and wanted to know why I was killing time under the platform. I told him I wasn't killing time."

Pity the Chicken

The *Frame Maker* reported that the employee picnic held in the summer of **1925** included a kittenball game, blindfold races, a "married ladies running race, any age," a "fat man's race, any age," a tug of war, a "ladies nail driving contest (ladies bring their own hammers)," wheelbarrow races, and an event called Catching the Chicken for married women only, with the chicken as the prize.

1. Ready to Serve
Avery Hokanson and the Andersen food service staff, shown here in the early 1950s.

2. The Cat Came Back
Cats shared the Andersen plant with employees until the arrival of motorized hauling equipment in the 1940s.

3. Picnic Time
While catching chickens is no longer a featured event, the Andersen employee picnic still ranks as one of the summer's highlights.

81

Betty and Bill Hulings

After they met over an animal dissection in a biology class at Carleton College in the mid-1930s, Mary Elizabeth "Betty" Andersen and A. D. "Bill" Hulings fell in love with each other, not with the idea of jointly working to shape the future of the Andersen Corporation. But in addition to marrying in 1938 and having a family, devoting their lives to Andersen is exactly what Betty and Bill went on to do.

After college, Betty roamed Europe for five months by car, taking in many of the grim political developments that foretold the outbreak of World War II. This experience gave her added perspective as she served on the Andersen board of directors for 60 years beginning in 1937. That same year Bill worked his first day at the Andersen Corporation, and few people guessed that he would soon marry the boss' daughter. Nepotism certainly did not help him as he unloaded lumber and counted screws.

Fred Andersen refused in principle to give preference to any family member. "Dad earned his way, sometimes in spades," says Bill's daughter Martha Kaemmer. "His brain was his asset, not the family he married into."

Bill was made purchasing agent in 1938, assistant production manager in 1941, vice president of production management in 1953, operations vice president in 1962, and treasurer in 1965. He became Andersen's president in 1968 when Earl Swanson moved to chairman of the executive committee. Bill absorbed many of the traditions of his predecessors, showing concern for his employees, maintaining an "open door" policy in his office, and even counseling workers on their marriages. He ended his Andersen career as chair of the executive committee, serving from 1975 to 1993.

Betty frequently joined Bill on business trips, representing Andersen at trade shows and other social functions. "The company was our life," says daughter Martha. "It was what we talked about at dinner and what Dad smelled like when he came home. His office was right across from the dip tank, but it was a good smell."

Betty and Bill generously supported many arts and educational institutions, including Carleton College, the Girl and Boy Scouts, and the Plymouth Music Series. Bill died in 1994 from complications of Parkinson's Disease, and many remember him as Andersen's finest organization builder — the founder of the company's Plant Engineering, Quality Control, and Personnel departments. Betty lived another six years, filling her life with her love of music, her family, her interest in the company, and the writing of her memoirs. Together Betty and Bill lived by the Biblical credo, "From those to whom much has been given, much shall be required." Their family's HRK Foundation continues to honor that spirit.

82

83

family

Hugh Andersen

The most enigmatic figure in the Andersen family, Hugh Andersen played an important role in the growth of the company during the **1940s**, '**50s**, and '**60s**. "He was an adventurer with vision, someone ahead of his time," remembers former executive Alan Johnson. Hugh grew frustrated by his inability to change Andersen in the ways he thought most important, though, and he eventually moved on to other activities.

Along with his sister Betty Andersen Hulings, Hugh was orphaned by the deaths of his parents in the early **1920s** and reared by his uncle Fred Andersen, president of the company. An athletic boy with an intense gaze, Hugh liked to roller skate through the empty expanses of the Andersen plant on weekends. He first became an Andersen employee before the U.S. entered World War II, supervising the construction of Andersen-built Stout houses for the U.S. military in Alaska.

Hugh served in the military during World War II and the Korean War, working at Andersen in the years between the conflicts. When his service was over, he did not return to Andersen employment. Fred Andersen dispatched Bill Hulings to Colorado in order to persuade Hugh to return to the company. He agreed to come back and went into the sales department. Torn between his desire to please his family and his need to make his own career choices, Hugh stayed more than a dozen years at Andersen, rising to sales manager and treasurer.

Despite his inner conflicts, Hugh was a well-liked and talented manager. He helped create the company's regional sales territories, overhauling a sales system that had been in place for decades. "He was a really good sales manager who loved to hunt," Johnson recalls. "When he was playing golf, he didn't care where the ball went — he just wanted to see it go far. He was a generous man who did a lot of good for people anonymously."

After leaving Andersen in the mid-**1960s**, Hugh operated and renovated the Pennington Hotel in Afton, Minn., later called the Afton House, and owned a restaurant in Lake Elmo. He frequently helped people whose lives were in disarray because of addictions or other problems. In **1966** he ran unsuccessfully for the Minnesota legislature.

Hugh remained on the Andersen board, however, until his death in **1977**. He left behind a rich legacy for Andersen and the community: his daughters, Christine, Carol (now deceased) and Sarah, who have made their own important contributions to Andersen Corporation, and the Hugh J. Andersen Foundation, which promotes independence, self-sufficiency, and human dignity throughout the St. Croix Valley.

Sarah Andersen

Sarah Andersen grew up in Bayport with the Andersen plant in her backyard and Andersen employees as her neighbors. She had no inkling as a child, or even through her early adulthood, that someday she would chair the company's board of directors.

Sarah is the daughter of Jane Krause and Hugh Andersen and granddaughter of Kitty and Fred Andersen. With her sisters Christine and Carol, she was reared in a household in which the Andersen Corporation loomed large but was rarely discussed. Hugh, who served as Andersen's sales manager and held several other positions in the company, raised Sarah to follow any career she chose but did not expect his children to assume the mantle of Andersen responsibility. Sarah finished her education at Carleton College with a B.A. in English literature and worked on the boards of several nonprofit organizations.

When Hugh died in 1977, Sarah's mother assumed his seat on the Andersen board and began bringing Sarah to shareholder meetings. "Then she passed away in 1981, and I asked for me or one of my sisters to have the family seat on the board," Sarah recalls. "I discovered that some of the executives were reluctant to take seriously the Andersens of my generation, because as women we had been kept distant from the inner workings of the company."

Sarah persisted and joined the board in 1982. "It was very interesting for me to see that at that time the board was a rubber stamp, a reward for seniority," she says. "It had very little to do. The executive committee was the real decision-making group."

Gradually, Sarah worked to strengthen the board. "I wanted the board to take responsibility. That's what a real governing body does," she says. She worked to reduce the size of the board, establish active committees, and balance the board membership among owners, management, and independent directors. The board began to focus on long-term planning and succession for the continued success of Andersen into the next generation.

Sarah was elected chair of the board in 1993. Since then, she has become one of the company's strongest proponents of change, immersing the board in the company's activities and helping strategize Andersen's resurgence after its doldrums of the 1990s. Once asked if changes in the company made her nervous, she replied, "No, it's the lack of change that makes me nervous."

She maintains a deep understanding of community and responsibility for one another. "Our products make people's homes and lives better," she says. "It's important to me that our business accomplishes something positive and is socially responsible."

86

87

The Quarter Century Club

In **1936** a group of five longtime Andersen employees piled into Fred Andersen's big sedan for a summer drive. This get-together of old-timers proved so enjoyable that the men vowed to make it an annual event. As the years went by, anyone with 25 years of service in the company was invited to join the group, which was named the Quarter Century Club.

By **1939** the number of members had climbed to nineteen. The Glengarry frequently hosted the annual meeting. Two women, Celestine Rowland and Mary Kilkelly, joined the group in **1944**. The membership reached 474 in **1977** and stood at 1,827 in **2003**.

Quarter Century Club membership is a great Andersen honor, but a select subgroup of the Club attained 50 years of service. They are Noble Roland, Elmer Lomnes, William Goulette, Jim Rowland, and Earl Swanson. Fred Andersen attained an incredible 75 years of service.

← 1

3

89

4

5

6

1. Quarter Century Club in 1942
Just six years old, the employee
organization was still small.
Fred Andersen is standing at left.

2. Quarter-Centurions
Quarter Century Club members
gather on the banks of the
St. Croix River.

3. Quarter Century Club Pin

4-6. All Together Now
Quarter Century Club events
through the years.

People

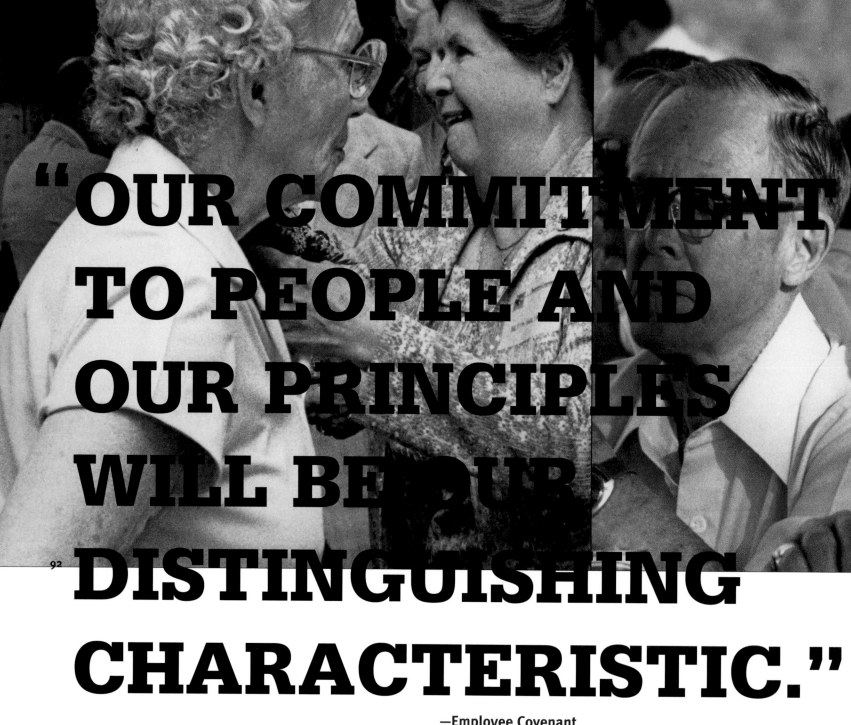

"OUR COMMITMENT TO PEOPLE AND OUR PRINCIPLES WILL BE OUR DISTINGUISHING CHARACTERISTIC."

—Employee Covenant

93

94

95

Customers

Today the people of Andersen Corporation benefit from a fantastic legacy: a 100-year-old tradition of caring for customers. During the Great Depression, when buying a house represented a real risk, Andersen reassured customers that only the rich could afford to jeopardize their investment with poor windows. Thirty years later the clear superiority of Perma-Shield and other Andersen products gave additional protection to customers. In the **1990s** when customers seeking peace of mind wanted worry-proof doors and windows, Andersen delivered. And now, as people become even more emotionally attached to their homes, Andersen offers beautiful products that fulfill their function in new ways that meet the complex demands of the 21st century. While the foundation of the Andersen brand remains constant — high quality products, business integrity, and beautiful design — generations of Andersen employees have learned to interpret and apply the brand in ways that help **customers** of their era. Whenever Andersen's approach to its business changes for the better, it happens because the company is responding to changes in the marketplace.

The Sales Force

Early in the company's history, Andersen's sales force consisted solely of Fred Andersen, who lugged frame parts over a wide area of Minnesota and Wisconsin. But after Hans Andersen's death in **1914**, the company needed Fred closer to home. Raymond Crowley stepped in as Andersen's first full-time sales representative, joining the company around **1916**. Crowley spent a great deal of his time on the road, introducing much of the Upper Midwest to Andersen frames.

By the time Crowley left less than ten years later, the sales force and its selling methods had undergone a complete transformation. The payroll included five full-time salesmen in **1924**. (One of them, Bob Nash, covered the entire eastern United States.) All had passed a tough set of tests, including a timed demonstration of nailing together a window frame. Anyone who could not assemble the frame in ten minutes, using exactly nineteen nails, had no future in sales.

These early sales representatives, and many who came later, approached their work with passion and did not treat their duties as just part of a regular job. Their work, keeping Andersen's name constantly before their customers, required unending effort in difficult circumstances. Living conditions on the road were not luxurious, and sales representatives sometimes shared hotel facilities with crooks and fugitives.

Through the difficult years of the Great Depression and into the **1940s**, the company focused its attention on the eastern and midwestern United States. In **1939** Andersen was selling to 40 states, nearly all east of the Rockies. Working in large territories, the sales force reported to a sales manager in Bayport. In **1959**, however, Andersen began to rethink this arrangement. Clare Stout was appointed Andersen's first field sales manager, with six regional sales managers reporting to him. "The regional sales managers had considerable experience and abilities," says Harold Meissner, the first sales manager to head a region. "They were the people in the field to go to for help. They would travel with a new sales representative and give him ideas on how to do calls. It was good to have somebody besides those in Bayport getting acquainted with customers."

The old sales model worked well until the **1990s**, a time of greater competition from other window makers and a decline in Andersen's market share. A more sophisticated way of identifying markets and finding solutions for customers led to a revamping of the company's sales approach. Changes were necessary because unlike in the past, Andersen's main market segments — remodelers, do-it-yourselfers, replacement window customers, custom

98

builders, and volume builders — now each demand a full range of Andersen products, from low-priced to super-premium windows and doors. In **2000** a great modernization occurred at an Andersen sales meeting in Tampa, Florida. "In a truly historic event, we moved from a manufacturer's representative model to more of a direct selling model," explains Jay Lund, senior vice president of sales. "It was all linked to our decision to take ownership of the customer." Sales representatives now specialize in building relationships with a specific kind of customer — such as builders, architects, or home-improvement retailers — rather than trying to be generalists who sell to distributors. "Since then, customers have had a single point of contact with Andersen, and our sales force is focused on customers, making them valued partners," Jay says. With this rebirth of intimacy in sales, Andersen uses different products, promotions, price points, and distribution methods to reach each customer category.

Andersen's sales force is now more expert and diverse than ever before. Women make up 10 percent of the group, and in **2001** the first woman joined Andersen's President's Club, an elite recognition for sales staff.

1. Sales Journal
An Andersen ledger from 1927 lists sales and commissions for each member of the company's sales force.

1

2

3

1. Sales Presentation Folder
Andersen sales staff used guides like this throughout the 1950s and '60s to learn selling tips and techniques.

2. Sales Posters
Printed by the thousands, these posters and many others like them sold builders and dealers on Andersen products.

3. 1965 Sales Meeting
The annual sales meeting gathered together in Bayport dozens of Andersen sales staff members from across the country.

Harold Meissner

Harold Meissner began his Andersen career in **1936** in the hardware department but made his biggest mark in sales. He was a life-long supporter of Andersen and passionate about the company.

In the mid-**1950s**, the company set up its first sales region, a 17-state area stretching from Florida to Kansas in which Andersen felt there was promise in establishing a regionally based and directed sales force. Harold, who had previously been Andersen's sales training manager, headed south and based himself in Atlanta in order to oversee the efforts of this fledgling enterprise. "There was so much territory to cover," he remembers. "We had to concentrate on the good markets in the region, to be in the markets where the money was." He made the experiment a success by launching a training program for distributors and dealers, and by focusing on the needs of customers in the region. Harold went on to serve as nationwide sales manager, vice president of sales, and executive vice president of marketing before he became president.

Like so many other Andersen leaders, Harold had put in his time in the trenches of the or-ganization. "When I started at Andersen, I remember clearly that my wage was 30 cents per hour," he says. "But Andersen was not a large company then, and I was interested in finding a better opportunity. Before World War II, I had the chance to come into the office in the order department. I took a pay cut of about five dollars a month in order to take that job."

After a couple of years in the military, Harold returned to Andersen and found a place in service work in the field. He first worked under Vern Bell in Illinois and Indiana, and he later took over the area when Vern was disabled in an auto accident. Later he headed the service region that included Ohio, Kentucky, and Tennessee.

Harold's presidency was distinguished by unprecedented sales growth, the refinement of the Perma-Shield product line, and the introduction of High-Performance glass. "I retired in **1992** from the presidency and from the board of directors," he says. "My, how the company has changed since then. There are new approaches to distribution and sales. But one thing has remained constant. As Fred Andersen always said, only the rich can afford to buy poor windows. Andersen is still making the best windows around." And the company is growing again.

102

Service

Several decades ago, Arvid Wellman and Harold Meissner, then Andersen's president and head of sales, met with a research consultant who asked how long Andersen windows should be expected to last in a home. Harold replied with a time span that astounded the consultant, who then realized that Andersen wants a lifetime relationship with its customers.

Servicing its products is an important part of that relationship. In the company's early years, members of the sales force serviced the products. With the later growth of the company, though, a full-time service staff was needed. In 1939 Herb Gardner became the first serviceman. During World War II, Gardner traveled for two days to reach a customer in Oklahoma whose window was disabled by a dust storm. The job took him twenty minutes to complete.

The 1970s and '80s proved trying times. Andersen had become the nation's first window manufacturer to use an insulated glass, made by Pittsburgh Plate Glass, that held gas between its two welded panes. A batch of freon pumped between the panes had been contaminated and turned blue when exposed to sunlight. Andersen immediately began a massive replacement program. Following that problem, customers began reporting cracks in the corners of certain Perma-Shield windows. Determined to repair or replace every flawed window, an overwhelmed Service Department fell behind in fixing the problem.

As a longterm result, however, Andersen and its customers benefited from this mishap. An overhaul of service procedures in the mid-1990s produced new ways by which Andersen gathers, diagnoses, and solves service problems. The company set up its first call center for customers and began using sophisticated computer tools that enable service representatives to diagnose nearly all problems with just five questions. A network of independent technicians and service agents contracted by retailers makes most repairs within a week. And Andersen's first written limited warranty clarifies the company's dedication to helping customers with problems.

Andersen's commitment to service was tested in 2001 with the recall of large numbers of 200 Series windows produced with potentially flawed tilt-latch mechanisms. "It was the only recall in our history, and we handled it well," says Mike Johnson, executive vice president and chief financial officer. "The efficient process we use to operate in a crisis is one of the factors that helps define Andersen's image."

"Andersen always strives to do it right the first time, and that effort is an important element of the Andersen brand," says company president Jim Humphrey. "But when customers experience problems, Andersen's promise is to resolve the issue in a way that exceeds customers' expectations."

104

1. 1993 Service Meeting

2-3. Visiting the Plant
Service employees of the 1990s visit Andersen manufacturing facilities in order to learn about new products and service techniques.

3

1

Spanning the Globe

Although Andersen began distributing its products to Canada in **1957** and to Japan in the mid-**1980s**, the company's first focused effort to build up its international business took place in the **1990s**. "We realized that we had to act quickly," remembers Ross Dahlin, general manager of international operations for Andersen. "In countries like Mexico, Korea, and England, construction was going on and they were looking for American products."

In **1994**, president and CEO Jerry Wulf led the company to explore international markets that lacked access to American-made windows and doors. Andersen has set up showrooms in 73 cities around the world and a network of 34 distributors in such countries as the United Kingdom, Mexico, China, Brazil, Korea, Poland, Turkey, and Taiwan. The company's emphasis on building good relationships with its business partners has brought hundreds of foreign building professionals each year to the U.S. to tour Andersen facilities. This investment pays off with orders for major building projects across the globe, involving such distribution partners as Black Millwork Co. in the United Kingdom and Ireland, R.C. Toemmerby in Denmark, VOMA in Poland, and Atlantis Muhendislik in Turkey.

The growth of the international business has not come easily, and the company has had to flexibly respond to obstacles. In **2002**, Chinese officials delayed shipments of Andersen products because of their new restrictions on wood pallets, which they feared might harbor troublesome beetles. With help from several U.S. government agencies, Andersen became one of the first American companies to meet the new pallet regulations. In the United Kingdom, where high quality windows and doors are traditionally not as highly valued as in the U.S., the company teamed with a local advertising agency to create new ad campaigns in the Queen's English.

In **1997** the International Division snared a record order for windows and patio doors to be installed in Marvel Star Iohno Golf Course clubhouse in Nasu, Japan. The project demanded standards of accuracy greater than most American orders. To prepare Andersen employees for this order, the International Division showed them travelogues about Japan and explained the Japanese cultural interest in accuracy. In the end, Andersen shipped the products, all with one-sixteenth-inch or one-thirty-second-inch tolerance, and everyone took pride in it.

1. Mexico
During the 1990s, Andersen entered many international markets, including Mexico, where Andersen products were installed in this upscale home.

2. Japanese Golf Course Clubhouse
One of Andersen's most demanding international projects of the 1990s was the clubhouse of the Marvel Star Iohno Golf Course.

106

107

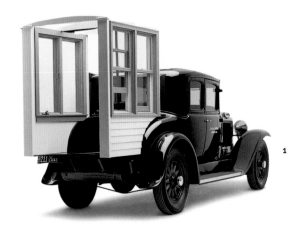

Andersen on Wheels

Over the past century, Andersen has owned a diesel locomotive and a fleet of trucks and semi trailer vans too numerous to count. But its most memorable vehicle by far was a Buick Series 129 automobile, Model 58, circa **1929**, of which only one or two photos survive.

The car, and the striking window display it carried, was the brainstorm of Jim Rowland, the company's longtime sales director. Rowland and the Buick traveled the country demonstrating the design and benefits of Andersen's Master Casement window and Narroline frame. In the early **1930s**, casement models had a reputation among architects and builders as troublesome windows — ones that would stick when damp or let in lots of air and moisture at other times. "With Jim's traveling demonstrator, we'd go into a city, park the Buick, and the really big sales job we had was to persuade an architect or builder to come outside," recalled Jim's brother, the late Joe Rowland, then a new member of the sales force. "Once he agreed to that, a demonstration spoke for itself."

The auto began its Andersen service a few years before Rowland converted it to a demonstrator. Fred Andersen bought it around **1930** for a road trip to California. Originally painted red, the car frequently toured Fred and his assistant Earl Swanson around the country. Rowland got his hands on it in **1932**, painted it black, and modified it to accommodate the window display.

The Buick became famous to people in the window industry, but no one knows how long the company used it or what happened to it afterward. Recently Andersen decided to bring it back.

Two employees, Ron Kuehn and Dave Swanson, tried to locate a nearly identical car. The task was difficult because only 734 Series 129s were built in **1929**. Finally in **1998** they found one for sale, a car with only 73,000 original miles and three owners. It had not been on the road for more than 40 years. In an extensive restoration, the car was reupholstered, repainted, and equipped with a rebuilt engine. By **1999** the Buick was fit for the road.

Carrying a display of vintage windows, the reborn Buick represents the company in parades and conventions, and is a part of Andersen's historical collection.

1. Andersen Buick Reproduction
Today a reproduction of the company's 1929 Buick has joined the company's service, appearing in parades and other special events.

2. Jim Rowland and the Andersen Buick
Andersen's sales director traveled countless miles in this auto during the 1930s. Jim's brother John is at the wheel.

3-4. Details from Restored Buick

108

3

4

2

109

customers

Jim Rowland, Joe Rowland, and John Rowland

Three brothers — Jim, Joe, and John Rowland — shaped, influenced, and directed Andersen's sales efforts from the **1920s** through the **1960s**. They grew up in Bayport, playing in piles of sawdust and working as teenagers in the sawmills. All three brothers (as well as their sister Celestine, who worked for several years in Andersen's accounting department) were good-natured, friendly, and connoisseurs of a good joke. At one point the Rowlands were Andersen's sole selling representatives in the entire northeastern United States, often staying on the road from Sunday evening through Saturday.

To the distributors, wholesalers, architects, builders, and lumberyard operators who formed the core of the company's clientele during those decades, the Rowlands were Andersen, the faces they attached to the Andersen brand.

Jim

Jim Rowland made his way to Andersen via jobs as a lumber camp clerk, an office clerk at a lumber company, and manager of a retail lumberyard in Rosemount, Minnesota. In **1919** Fred Andersen hired Jim as the manager of the Andersen Yard Company, a retail lumber operation. He quickly established himself as an excellent salesman, relying on his people skills to establish a "belly to belly" bond with his customers. Fred promoted him to sales manager in **1930**. "I never had any desire to be sales manager," Jim said years later. "I hadn't done any traveling... [but] Fred said I was going to be sales manager,

and I didn't want to turn him down." His first task was to join Fred and Earl Swanson on a 3,000-mile trip to introduce the eastern U.S. to the company's new Master Frame.

Switchboard operator Marilyn Peterson called Jim "a short, chunky Irishman - cigar in his mouth, a twinkle in his eye, and little burn holes in his necktie." (He smoked so many cigars that his secretary was able to get a steam iron and a ring by redeeming thousands of the cigar bands he gave her.) He grew into a man known around the country for his love of people, refusal to drink alcohol or travel in airplanes, quick wit and energy, and eagerness to prove that he represented the world's finest window products.

Jim, who eventually rose to vice president of sales, had a legendary sense of humor. When orders were scarce during the Great Depression, he once was chatting aboard a train with his seatmate about the home building slow down. "By the way," Jim said, "what do you sell?" "Secondhand locomotives," was the reply. Said Jim: "Well, I guess I'm not too bad off after all."

"There was a prince. Yes, Jim Rowland was a great man," remembered former president and board chair Earl Swanson. "He didn't know very much about lumber. He didn't know a whole lot about windows, but he knew a great deal about people and he was a real salesman, a good one. Everybody loved Jim Rowland."

Joe

Joe Rowland originally worked in the Andersen plant and on the order desk. He joined the sales force in **1925**, assuming responsibility the following year for the sales territory stretching from Washington, D.C., to Florida. He later took charge of territories in New York, Ohio, Tennessee, Kentucky, and New England.

"At the beginning," he later remembered, "we traveled mostly by train. I was often riding a sleeper two or three nights a week." He traveled with his brother Jim during the Great Depression, when Jim had his famous traveling demonstration of casement windows mounted on the tail end of a Buick. "In Charleston, Virginia, we parked the Buick at an angle, and while Jim was demonstrating to some architects and builders, a big crowd gathered. Next thing we knew, a cop pushed through the audience and announced, 'Get this thing outa here — you're blocking the streetcar line!'"

Joe's career with Andersen lasted more than 40 years.

John

John Rowland, taller than his brothers, joked that he was born in the same month as George Washington and Abraham Lincoln, "the only difference being that they were lucky enough to be born on holidays and I wasn't." After serving in World War I, he came to work for Andersen in **1921**. He entered the sales force and for several years held the entire western U.S. as his sales territory. Later he had responsibility for southern New York, Connecticut and Massachusetts. In **1939** he returned to Bayport to succeed his brother Jim as sales manager.

John's style was quieter and gentler than that of his brothers, and his customers knew him as absolutely trustworthy and honest. "When he told you something would be done, you didn't even need to shake hands on it," said one. His Andersen coworkers liked to tease him about his lack of a wife, but all that ended in **1932** when he married May. "She was making baked beans, one time, and John questioned her as to how she was preparing them," recalls Nyda Swanson, Earl's widow. "May lost her temper and said, 'John Rowland, you sell the windows and I'll bake the beans!'"

John, whose son John Jr. is retired from Andersen and a member of the Quarter Century Club, died suddenly from a heart attack in **1954**.

1. Jim Rowland
Andersen's longtime sales director was known nationwide for his cigar and quick wit.

2. Joe Rowland
Joe served Andersen for more than 40 years, working enormous sales territories.

3. John Rowland
John followed Jim as sales manager in 1939 and made his own mark as a trustworthy company representative.

111

1

3

2

4

112

Diary of a Sales Manager

For nearly 40 years, Jim Rowland kept diaries of his personal and professional life. They show a hard working man who never tired of taking a genuine interest in the people he met.

May 19, 1930: "Left Bayport 7:10 a.m. for Mason City. Got addresses of new jobs using 601 Master Frame.

Met Mr. Sturm, carpenter doing finishing work. He had put in Master Frame on another job — very well satisfied. Said if Andersen frame was installed as it should be, it was worth 50 percent more than any competitive frame. He sure would use them if he was building a home of his own."

September 24, 1932, Ferguson, Missouri: "Met Mr. C.J. Harris. Harris figuring house for Mr. Emery W. Chase, a St. Louis lawyer. Demonstrated casement to Chase and his wife. Mr. Chase figuring on steel. Asked me to show casement to Mr. Julius C. Tarling, his architect. Mr. Tarling very much impressed."

February 26, 1940, Mansfield, Ohio: "Twenty-five contractors at our evening meeting. Called on the editor of the *Mansfield Free Press* and talked to him about running a story about our new unit."

1. No Bail
Members of the St. Croix Lumbermen's Association arranged a mock "arrest" of Jim Rowland.

2. Jim Rowland and Business Partner
Jim posed with a customer in 1951 while giving a sales presentation.

3. The Lighter Side
Jim sometimes donned fanciful costumes for trade association meetings.

4. In the Factory
An informal portrait, circa 1960, of (left to right) Bill Hulings, Henry Rickers, Earl Swanson, Jim Rowland, Bill Kemer, and Fred Andersen.

5. Sales Manager at Work
Jim Rowland shows the advantages of the Andersen Locked Sill-Joint.

A Public Face

As Andersen grew during its first hundred years, the art of advertising grew along with it. Entirely new forms of advertising were born during Andersen's initial century, such as television commercials, and the company took advantage of them. At the same time the goals of Andersen's advertising sharpened in sophistication, becoming more a way to build a strong brand image than a method of communicating detailed information about products.

Don Wilson, a former high school teacher and county agricultural agent who was hired as the company's first advertising manager in **1925**, realized that it was most important for Andersen to establish a reputation among those who could place its products into house plans — builders, contractors, and architects. "We were not ready to go into consumer publications then," Wilson said. He developed a series of detailed, illustrated brochures, including cross-section cutaways. He also directed the production of Andersen's catalogue of **1926** — the first compendium of frame and window details ever made.

In **1933** Andersen began a relationship with one of its most important business suppliers, Campbell-Mithun, Inc., a Minneapolis advertising agency. Beginning with an initial assignment to produce promotional aprons and pencils for carpenters, Campbell-Mithun has gone on to create advertising for Andersen for another 70 years.

During World War II, the company faced an advertising dilemma: How could it best market its windows when Andersen was heavily engaged in non-window war production and home construction had ground to a halt? Campbell-Mithun devised the solution, a home-planner's scrapbook that allowed Americans to build their fantasy house, at least on paper. The scrapbook included pouches for pictures, plans, fabric and carpeting samples, and sketches. Priced at 50 cents and embossed with the purchaser's name, the scrapbook sold more than 350,000 copies — even one to Judy Garland.

Meanwhile, Andersen added public tours and other face-to-face strategies to its marketing arsenal. The touring tradition began in the late-**1930s**, when Andersen inaugurated a Ladies Day inspection tour at the Bayport plant. Production shut down for part of an afternoon so that the work crew's wives, mothers, girlfriends, and female neighbors could see for themselves how the factory's then all-male employees spent their day. Today the Andersen tour is a popular, even moving, experience for nearly 8,000 customers and community members each year. "Seeing how Andersen operates leaves a lasting impression," says Jay Lund, senior vice president of sales and logistics. "And that has been true for 100 years."

Other events helped associate Andersen with a culture of hospitality. Starting in the **1920s**, distributors and other business suppliers have come to Bayport for meetings that emphasized the shared pleasures of food, cards, and music. During the **1960s**, a country-western music group called the Friendly Valley Boys, made up of Andersen employees

114

Look both ways
before crossing the room.

2

(Dave Speich, Dave Croft, Jerry Wulf, Don Garofalo, and Wendell Belisle), serenaded commercial customers at weekly fondue dinners at the Lowell Inn in Stillwater, Minnesota. Long after the food was forgotten, the music continued ringing in their ears. Customers never forgot the friendliness that Andersen offered them, and it helped cement relationships that lasted for generations. This warmth was one of the earliest ingredients of Andersen's distinctive brand image and it continues today.

In partnership with Campbell-Mithun, Andersen has spent the past 70 years formulating and refining Andersen's brand image — without question one of the company's most valuable assets and the attribute that sets it apart from its competitors. As a result of this work, Andersen's name conveys a powerful message to customers, a message far more important than the value of any single window or door. "The most consistent aspect of the brand has been quality," said the late Dave Harvey, a Campbell-Mithun executive who worked on the Andersen account for 25 years. "Quality relates to products, but it also relates to the ways in which Andersen handles problems. During the 1970s, when the gas pumped between panes by a glass supplier turned thousands of Andersen windows blue, there was never any question of what the company would do. It worried about the brand image first, didn't wait for complaints, and replaced all of the windows. The supplier later said it would have gone broke if it hadn't been for Andersen's aggressive response."

Over the decades, Andersen's advertising, marketing, and product development have strengthened the other facets of the Andersen brand: beauty, outstanding workmanship, and the company's contributions to the comforts of home. Andersen is currently making a major marketing effort to more strongly connect windows and doors with customers' feelings about their home. After a century in business, Andersen owns the strongest brand image of any window or door maker in the world. "In these early years of the twenty-first century, our brand is more important than it's ever been before," says Phil Donaldson, senior vice president of marketing and business development. "What *Long Live the Home* tells customers is that Andersen is a permanent part of the beauty, comfort, and security their homes provide."

115

1. Branded
A wood brand used to mark Andersen frames of the 1920s and '30s.

2. Long Live the Home
The company's most recent marketing campaign stresses Andersen's role in making a house a home.

1

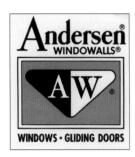

2

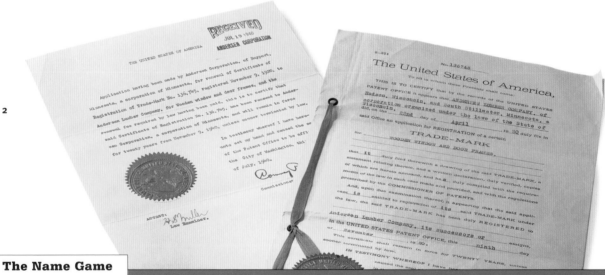

The Name Game

Andersen has used three corporate names in its history: Andersen Lumber Company (**1903**), Andersen Frame Company (**1929**), and, after the success of its complete window units, Andersen Corporation (**1937**).

In addition, the company created an effective new term in **1944** with the introduction of the Andersen Windowalls trademark. The Campbell-Mithun advertising agency devised this name after observing that Andersen windows were so weather tight that they almost functioned as walls. Another well-known Andersen advertising slogan, "Only the Rich Can Afford Poor Windows," derived from a sentence in a speech Fred Andersen delivered in **1939** to a meeting of jobbers and salesmen.

1. A Parade of Logos
The development of the Andersen logo shows the company's progression from a maker of window frames to supplier of solutions for buyers of windows and doors.

2. Trademark Registration
Paperwork giving Andersen ownership of its company trademarks in 1920 and 1940.

3. Andersen Windowalls Advertisements
"Windowalls" was one of Andersen's earliest attempts to create a brand image that suggested beauty and craftsmanship.

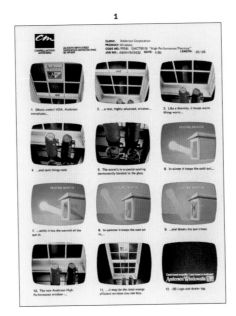

1

2

3

4

Hitting the Small Screen

Although television has always had its critics, Andersen is not one of them. The company has benefited tremendously from its TV advertising, which began in **1978**. The first commercials, which were produced for dealers for local airings, were shot on Fred Andersen's front lawn. Then, starting in **1981**, came a stream of commercials produced by Andersen for a national viewership. The first of these spots featured actual Andersen employees and scenes from the Bayport plant to convey the company's pride in its craftsmanship. "They turned out better than we expected," remembers Joe Arndt, Andersen's marketing director at the time. "We wanted the commercials to do several things, to excite our trade audience and our distributors and retail lumber dealers, but the main objective was to excite our own employees." Employees saw the premiere of the commercial at the annual profit sharing party, "and the excitement that came out that day was unreal," Arndt adds. "We also found that the ads substantially increased the public's awareness of Andersen. Later, when we experimentally went off TV for a while, we discovered a direct drop off in the public's recall of Andersen. TV allowed us to strengthen the Andersen brand," Arndt says. "It's an investment in the future."

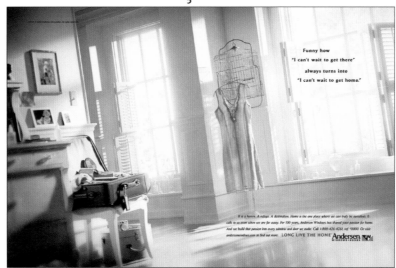

5

Funny how
"I can't wait to get there"
always turns into
"I can't wait to get home."

LONG LIVE THE HOME Andersen

They'll be around long enough
for your furniture to go out of style.
And come back in again.

LONG LIVE THE HOME Andersen

Be Sincere

119

Years ago, Ralph Campbell, a founder of the advertising agency Campbell-Mithun, Inc., recalled a meeting he attended with Fred Andersen and a magazine representative who wanted to sell ads to Andersen. "The rep commented, 'I remodeled my house recently, and when my wife chose another brand of window, I told her to go to hell, and insisted on Andersen,'" Campbell related. "Then he made his 20-minute pitch about the wonders his magazine could perform, and looked expectantly at Fred for a few words of approval.

"All Fred said was, 'Did you really tell your wife to go to hell?'"

1. Television Storyboard
Storyboards showing the images and messages included in a commercial became a common sight at Andersen once television advertising began in earnest in the 1980s.

2-4. Film Set
The shooting of an Andersen promotional film — not a commercial — in the 1960s.

5. Home
The company's most recent advertising has emphasized the comforts of home.

customers

120

**1-2. New York World's Fair
Model Home**
Andersen windows went into this
"home of the future" displayed
at the 1939 World's Fair.

3. Idea House
Another "house of the future,"
designed and built in 1941 at
Walker Art Center in Minneapolis,
that used Andersen windows.

122

Rapsons' Glass Cube.
(54 Andersen Windows and 24 Andersen Gliding Doors)

Designing his own weekend home was a lot tougher than award-winning architect Ralph Rapson thought.

Mainly because a conventional retreat just wouldn't do. He wanted a place that would allow him to take advantage of the picturesque Apple River Valley. But one that would not interfere with the valley's natural woodland beauty.

So Mr. Rapson designed a transparent home to permit continuity of nature throughout the house, when experienced from both inside and out.

His vehicle for bringing the idea to life? Andersen® Perma-Shield® Windows and Gliding Doors.

Mr. Rapson was impressed by their solid, sturdy construction and neat, trim lines.

And Mrs. Rapson liked their smooth, silent, easy operation.

The Rapsons will have plenty of time away from window chores to enjoy their home, too.

Because Perma-Shield Windows and Gliding Doors are made of wood and sheathed in long-life rigid vinyl that doesn't chip, crack or peel. Doesn't rust, pit or corrode.

And double-pane insulating glass eliminates storm window bother.

So, whether you're constructing a weekend retreat or an everyday building, use Perma-Shield Windows and Gliding Doors.

For more details, see Sweet's File 8P. Or contact your Andersen Distributor. His name is on the back cover.

Rapsons' Glass Cube.
Apple River Valley, Wisc.
Architect: Ralph Rapson, F.A.I.A.

1-3. Rapson's Glass Cube
The modernist architect Ralph Rapson specified Andersen windows for the "glass cube" he designed for his own use in 1974 near Amery, Wisconsin. Rapson never intended to build a glass house, but every time he drew a wall his wife complained it would block a view of the Apple River and the surrounding meadows. "I tried to use standard off-the-shelf materials, to make it economical," Rapson said.

Distribution

They came to Bayport from 13 states aboard a chartered Pullman sleeping car. They toured the Andersen plant, played golf, dined at the White Pine Inn, discussed window construction and sales, went to the movies, and played cards. At the end of three packed days in **1925**, the first national conference of Andersen's distributors had brought the company closer to 36 of its most important business allies.

From Andersen's earliest years, the company has never underestimated the importance of its distribution network. For decades, Andersen distributed its products only through wholesalers, who in turn passed the products to individual dealers who sold to contractors and builders. Products moved through four stages of distribution before reaching the people who would use Andersen products. There were no exceptions. When Fred Andersen wanted windows for his vacation property, he bought them at full retail price from an Andersen dealer who had obtained them through normal channels from a wholesaler.

Times change, though, and so have the ways in which Andersen delivers products to customers. Between **1988** and **1992**, the company's sales of window units fell by nearly a third. The distribution system, now obsolete, was partly responsible for the decline. There were simply too many competing distributors with overlapping territories. At the same time, "there was a real adversarial relationship between Andersen and its largest distributors," remembers Vic Springer, director of the

Andersen customer development organization who previously served for 25 years at Morgan Products, Ltd., then one of Andersen's largest distributors. These conflicts made it difficult for the company's partners to do business with Andersen.

Seeing a crisis that could cripple the company, Andersen restructured its distribution system. Morgan Products, together with Adam Wholesalers, Inc., another independent distributor it had just acquired, accounted for a significant part of Andersen's distribution network. Deeming that this was too much of its business to leave independent, Andersen purchased Morgan in **1999**. Along with Independent Millwork, Inc., another independent distributor Andersen acquired in **1999**, these businesses were reborn as Andersen Logistics, an Andersen subsidiary created to take costs out of the distribution system, improve dealer margins, streamline distribution, and bring Andersen closer to its customers. As a result of additional consolidation over the last few years, Andersen now owns more than half of its distribution channel. This gives the company more direct control over how it takes products to market and makes it easier for customers to do business with Andersen.

Meanwhile, many of Andersen's distributors, such old allies as Brockway-Smith Co., Black Millwork Co., Inc., Kellogg Wholesale Building Supply, and Hampton Distribution Companies,

124

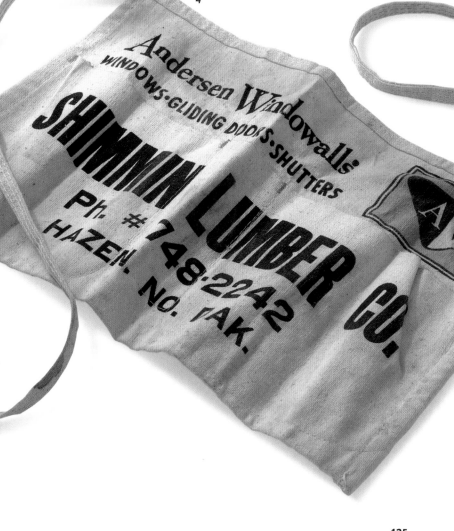

gained aligned distribution agreements for their geographic areas. Sadly, Andersen had to end its relationships with many longtime distributors — a bittersweet result of the necessary changes. Andersen also developed a closer relationship with The Home Depot, the nation's largest chain of home improvement stores, and, in turn, Andersen became the retailer's preferred window and patio door provider, establishing direct sales, service and delivery. It's now easier for all categories of customers to do business with Andersen. "In the past Andersen's weakness was how hard it was for builders and other customers to deal with us," says Vic Springer. "Now Andersen usually has a direct relationship with them."

There were risks involving the shouldering of long-term debt and the disturbance of old ways of doing things, always an emotional upheaval for employees. But the dangers of taking no action, of making no change, were far higher. The old means of doing business distanced Andersen from its customers — a fatal flaw for a company determined to increase its market share and serve its customers seamlessly. "During the 1980s the industry was changing quickly, and we were out of step," says Jay Lund, senior vice president of sales and logistics. "The largest of our customers were dealing directly with manufacturers. Then came the dark years when we lost customers and market share. We had to reinvent ourselves or vanish."

1. Andersen Trucks
The company's large fleet of trucks and trailers perform double duty as transporters of products and bearers of Andersen's marketing messages.

2. Lumber Dealer
Photographed in 1927, family members Leonard, Kenneth, and J.L. Howe of the Carrington Lumber Company in North Dakota received their Andersen products from a network of jobbers and distributors.

3. Lumber Company Advertising
A lumber retailer's handbill from 1924 promotes the Andersen line.

4. Promotional Apron
For decades, carpenter's and homebuilder's aprons have carried the Andersen logo.

1

1. First Time Together
A group portrait from Andersen's first convention of distributors in 1925, which included representatives from 36 companies.

2. Retailer's Window Display
A 1939 display at Gratoit Lumber and Coal Company of Detroit prominently showed an example of the Andersen casement window.

SEE THE MOST BEAUTIFUL WINDOW
RICA..... *The Andersen Casement*......

SEE HOW
EASY
IT IS TO CLEA

MODERNIZE!

ARCHITECTURALLY
CORRECT
FOR ANY TYPE HOME

127

Andersen
WOOD CASEMENTS
EATHERTIGHT LEAKPROOF
CONV ENT

NO AIR
INFILTRATION

SG ASBESTOS SIDIN
CEMENT

customers

1

1. Trade Show Display
Consumers examine the
Andersen product line at a trade
show display of the 1950s.

2. Trade Show Dazzle
Andersen's contemporary trade
show exhibits display a
dazzling mix of new products and
innovative future technologies.

Since 1903, Andersen has worked with professionals
like you to transform wishes into walls and
roofs and memories. In this, our Centennial
year, we continue to introduce new products
that set your homes apart in an increasingly
competitive marketplace. LONG LIVE THE HOME

customers

1

2

3

130

The Anderson Corp.
Bayport,
Minnesota

MRS. MARGARET RICHMOND
3166 WEST 11TH ST.
CLEVELAND, OHIO

Enclose find .50¢ for
"Scrapbook for our new Home."
Print name on it.
"Gene + Anne Brumlee"
Thank you
I enjoy my book so much
I am ordering one for a friend
Mrs. a Richmond
3166 W 11 street
Cleveland, Ohio

4

1-3. Home Planners' Scrapbook
The company's scrapbook
for home planners carried the
Andersen name to tens of
thousands of Americans just
waiting for the end of World War
II to begin their lives anew
and build a home.

4. Scrapbook Order Request
The letter and payment of a
customer in Ohio who wanted to
order the Andersen scrapbook.

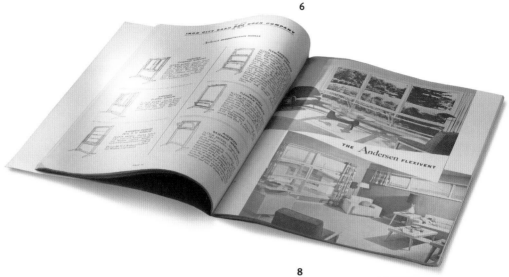

6

7　8　9

1. Promotional Poster
Builders were also the frequent audience for Andersen's promotional materials of the 1930s and '40s.

2. Service Van
Andersen's Service Department dates back to the 1930s.

3. Retail Display
A retailer's display on Park Avenue in New York City, shown here in 1940, promotes the new Andersen Horizontal Gliding Window.

4. Making a Delivery
Lumberyard workers load Andersen windows for a delivery in 1952.

5. Promotional Cards
Retailers used these cards during the 1920s to inform builders and other customers of the benefits of using Andersen frames.

6. Andersen Product Catalogue
In 1926 Andersen issued the nation's first catalogue of frame and window details. This catalogue from the 1940s served as a window bible to builders of its time, just as today's catalogues do now.

7. "We Use Andersen Windows"
Homebuilders have long known that Andersen products can help sell houses. Here a developer demonstrates the Beauty-Line window, circa 1955.

8. The Window Goes In
A homebuilder's crew installs Horizontal Gliding windows in a Minneapolis house around 1950.

9. Distribution Group
Andersen employees now over-see the wholesale distribution of more than half of the company's sales volume.

Tales from Customers

Many of the best Andersen stories come from customers, the people who live their lives around Andersen products. Here's a sampling of recent stories that customers have felt compelled to send along.

The Telemarketer Hangs Up

A customer in Grove City, Ohio, writes to say that a telemarketer selling replacement windows recently called him and asked what kind of windows were already installed. The customer explained that he had a ten-year-old home with original Andersen windows. "When I said, 'Andersen,' the telemarketer hung up on us," the customer declares. "Must have known he was wasting his time."

Best Bang for the Buck

When a customer asked a window cleaner in Telford, Pennsylvania, for suggestions on energy efficient window replacements for a 1952 home, he recommended Andersen windows. "I see all types of windows in my business every day, and as far as I'm concerned, Andersen gives the best bang for your buck," the window cleaner told the customer. He then pointed out that the original windows had given more than 50 years of service, and that it would be a shame to replace them with inferior windows. "And then, as I looked closely at their existing windows,

I saw Andersen written on the hardware!" he says. "Do you believe it? I said, 'If you are going to replace these windows, use Andersen windows and get another fifty-plus years.'"

Brother and Sister Operation

A customer in Pacific City, Oregon, wanted to find insulated inserts for Andersen windows that had been installed in his house during the 1970s. "Now I know that products twenty-plus years old are not supported — not my furnace, my fireplace insert, or my kitchen range. So my effort to fix my windows was to go to a glass shop to see about having the inserts made," the customer says. "When I mentioned that they were Andersen windows and the person whipped out an 800 number, I should have known there was something strange going on." The toll-free number connected him with Andersen's customer service center, where the customer expected to run a gauntlet of recorded messages. Instead, an agent explained how to find the model number of his window and how to measure them. Then the agent asked the customer to call her back with the information necessary to order the inserts. "I've been thinking about this a lot, and I've got it figured out," the customer writes. "You're not really a big company, but probably just two people, probably a sister and brother. She answers the phone and he makes the windows. And probably not very many windows, otherwise you couldn't be interested in dealing with twenty-year-old products and the customers that went with them."

Attention to Detail

A Renewal by Andersen customer in San Francisco, California, is a retired plastic surgeon, "someone who truly understands and appreciates the importance of anticipation and attention to detail that is required for excellent results," he writes. So when the Renewal installation crew arrived at his condominium, he was hoping for exemplary service. He got it. The replacement windows reduced noise from the outside, looked wonderful, and satisfied his neighbors who expected uniformity with the other windows in his building. He writes that he has recommended Renewal to three friends. "You listened to us, you came up with the solutions, you hired the best, and, having already received three calls after the job to make sure we were happy, you followed up. We are more than satisfied and 'we're glad we did it!'" he says.

A Welcome Fax

In Paris, Missouri, a customer needed help. In her mother's home, an Andersen window originally installed in 1972 had come apart at the sash. The customer had an identical window that had been removed a few years earlier for remodeling, and she wanted to know how to replace the damaged sash with the sash from the other window. Not expecting much, the customer called Andersen's customer support and explained the situation. The agent promised to look for an information sheet that would show how to replace the sash, and he promised to fax it to the customer when he found it. Two days later, "to my surprise a fax came through with the information that the agent had promised to try and find," the customer writes. "I was ecstatic that someone had actually taken the time to look for information on windows that were at least thirty years old. I followed the instruction sheet and successfully exchanged windows."

Saved from Fire

A fire destroyed the neighboring home of a customer in North Irwin, Pennsylvania. Six feet away from the blaze stood the customer's house and a wall full of Andersen windows. "The intensity of the fire melted the plastic grids and my vinyl blinds on the inside of the windows," the customer writes, "but not one of the four windows facing the intense fire broke or cracked for that matter. While our home suffered cosmetic damage, our Andersen windows prevented our home from being completely destroyed. Needless to say we are not disappointed and today we are especially grateful. Your product lives up to its reputation."

135

Andersen Sales Summary

YEAR	SIGNIFICANCE	YEARS BETWEEN MILESTONE
1922	$1 MILLION SALES MARK	28
1950	$10 MILLION SALES MARK	23
1973	$100 MILLION SALES MARK	23
1977	$250 MILLION SALES MARK	4
1984	$500 MILLION SALES MARK	7
1988	$1 BILLION SALES MARK	4
2002	$2 BILLION SALES MARK	14

Andersen Net Sales Chart

(in millions)

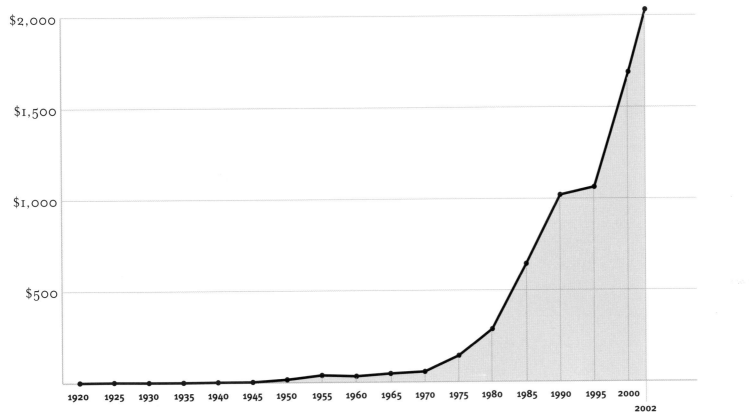

137

customers

Environment

"MEETING THE NEEDS OF THE PRESENT, WITHOUT COMPROMISING THE NEEDS OF THE FUTURE."

—Don Garofalo

141

142

143

Products

Imagine being a hundred years old. Imagine wanting to retire, rest on your laurels, and allow someone else to do the hard work of creating and innovating. You're imagining something completely foreign to the experience of Andersen Corporation. Every thirty years or so — even more frequently in recent times as customers demand an accelerated pace of change — the company has reinvented itself. The first change was the introduction of two-bundled frame packages in **1905**. In the **1930s** Andersen ceased making window frames and began manufacturing complete windows. Later, vinyl-clad windows and doors replaced all-wood **products** as Andersen's most important products. And with the passage of more time, Andersen was reborn as a company that has diversified its product line and revolutionized its distribution methods in order to better serve its customers and grow its business. This reinvention occurs with such regularity we should expect it, but it always requires strong leadership to make it happen.— In taking part in this drama, Andersen is responsible for many important innovations that changed the industry: bundled frames, complete and assembled windows, the acceptance of vinyl as a building material, energy efficient and environmentally sound products, and the use of new composite materials. In Andersen's hands, different really does mean better.

The First Products: 1903 – the 1920s

Before Hans Andersen and his sons launched their window frame manufacturing business in 1903, accurately made window frames were as rare as flawless diamonds. Local carpenters, lumberyards, and millwork shops built most frames as they were needed, and the results were often unsatisfactory. Air and moisture leaks, not to mention rotting and damage to the frames, were common.

Hans and his family invented their company on the bedrock of a major innovation: high quality window frames mass produced in standardized sizes. "We adopted our own standard details, while many manufacturers would make anybody's detail," said Ernie Madsen, who joined the company in 1923 and ran the Andersen foundry from 1930 to 1940. "That was the success of this company — standardization, no deviation."

And that standardization was at a very high level because — nine years before automaker Henry Ford came up with the idea — it allowed Andersen to benefit from mass production and the use of interchangeable parts. Andersen's earliest products — most of which were white pine frames for casement and double-hung windows — were renowned for the accuracy of their construction, their low cost, and their high level of workmanship. In only ten minutes, a carpenter could assemble and install a frame.

Andersen also experienced the disadvantages of standardization. In such cities as Philadelphia, Boston, Washington, and Baltimore, where local custom dictated unique window sizes, the company was shut out of the market. It took decades for these cities to shake off their solitary building practices and open themselves to Andersen products.

Elsewhere, though, Andersen quickly contributed to the standardization of the American window opening. The result was that total sales of Andersen frames reached 1 million in 1915. Sales accelerated after that, with the company reaching its next milestone of 2 million total units sold in 1919 and 3 million in 1922. By 1924, Andersen was making more than a million frames each year, and in 1929 it ranked as the world's largest specialized window frame factory.

Different and Better

Two-Bundle Packaging

Andersen developed the most innovative and efficient frame distribution method of its time, the "two-bundle" method of packaging. Using this system, which Hans Andersen did not believe was patentable, the company produced a bundle of eleven sets of horizontal frame parts and a second bundle of eleven sets of vertical parts.

Every Andersen frame could be built from a combination of these 121 horizontal and vertical parts, without any additional cutting or trimming. Just as important, dealers could supply every Andersen frame to customers by stocking only the two bundles, which each weighed less than 20 pounds.

1. Standard Window Brochures
The company's earliest
frame brochures emphasized
the product's high quality,
weather-tightness, and ease
of installation.

2. Early Standard Frame
This Andersen frame, installed in
the summer of 1905 in a house
in Hudson, Wisconsin, remained
in place for many years.

148

1-3. Standard Frame Bundles
One of Hans Andersen's greatest innovations was his development of the frame bundle, an assortment of horizontal and vertical sections from which jobbers and builders could assemble finished frames in 121 different sizes.

AUDITOR

149

products

150

1-2. 1920 and 1922 Standard Frame Catalogues
Andersen's catalogues of the early 1920s were wrapped in elegant, faux leather covers.

3. Standard Frame Advertising Series
These ads were among many that Andersen placed in a variety of building trade magazines of the 1920s.

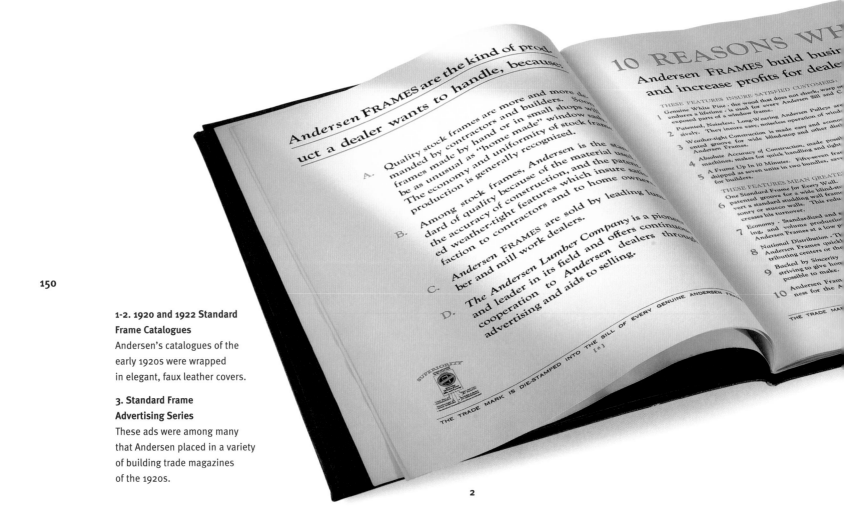

2

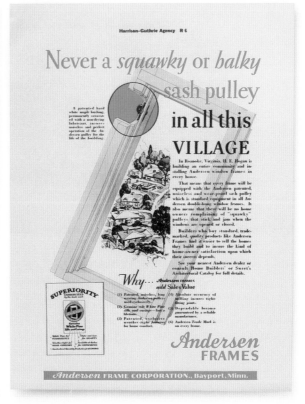

151

Evolving Products: The 1920s and 1930s

In September 1928, 17-year-old Earl Swanson, then Fred Andersen's assistant, set out on a long journey in his employer's six-cylinder Packard. He was driving alone from Bayport to Glendora, California, where Fred was caring for his ill wife. In eight days Earl made it to the west coast, having survived heavy storms and horrendous road conditions. Upon his arrival, Earl accompanied Fred to a series of business meetings. Unknown to both men, however, was the importance of the discussions they would have while driving together on their business calls. Casually and unexpectedly, Fred and Earl began talking about a new Andersen product that would revolutionize the window business.

Fred began by telling Earl about a conversation he'd had on the train out to California with an official of the Forest Products Laboratory in Wisconsin. That man "told Fred he might do well to put less emphasis on white pine and more on improving his design," Earl later related, "such things as increasing the slope of the sill, to lengthen the life of the product by shedding water more effectively." Earl and Fred discussed that idea at length, and they decided to think more about improving the design of their frames. About six months later, in a hotel in Portland, Oregon, "I attempted to put on a piece of brown wrapping paper — using a portable drawing board I carried with me — the first full presentation of a window frame which was later labeled 601, the first Master Frame drawing," Earl said.

The Master Frame for casement windows was ready for production in 1930. Although it was still sold unassembled, it differed from the company's earlier frames — as well as the products of all other frame manufacturers — in several ways. First, the frame was the first to use the Locked Sill-Joint, an ingeniously designed meeting of the sill and the jamb that provided a virtually leak-proof joint. Second, the slope of the sill was twice as steep as in most frames, making it much easier for rain to run off. In addition, the Master Frame was Andersen's first product in years not to be built from White Pine; the priming of joints with aluminum paint allowed the company to instead use less expensive Ponderosa Pine.

The result was a remarkably airtight frame, one that engineers at the University of Wisconsin found reduced air leakage by 53 percent over customary frames. In 1931, Andersen followed with a version of the Master Frame using new phosphor bronze weather strips, which reduced air leakage even more.

To promote the Master Frame, Andersen held meetings around the country with contractors, dealers, and architects. The Great Depression sent home construction into a tailspin, but slowly the Master Frame gained an appreciative market. Andersen discontinued production of the Master Frame in 1938 in order to focus on producing preassembled windows.

1. Master Frame Brochure
From the start, the weather-tightness of the Master Frame was its main selling point.

2-4. Master Frame Advertising
Andersen gave dealers Master Frame ad samples that they could customize for their local publications.

5. Master Frame Research and Memos
The company invested thousands of hours in designing and researching the Master Frame as well as investigating its potential markets.

Different and Better

The Locked Sill-Joint
The Andersen Master Frame was the first to use the Locked Sill-Joint, an ingeniously fashioned design element that had never before been built into a window frame. Fitting together like pieces of a jigsaw puzzle, the sill and the jamb formed a joint that was virtually impenetrable by water.

154

1. Cross-Section of Joint
Conversations between Fred Andersen and Earl Swanson launched the development of the ingenious Locked Sill-Joint.

2-3. Master Frame Literature
The Locked Sill-Joint was nearly impervious to leakage, according to the company's literature.

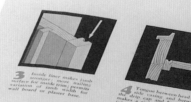

2

Andersen
MASTER FRAMES

DETAIL CATALOG NO. 46

manufactured by
ANDERSEN CORPORATION
BAYPORT, MINN.

3

LOCKED SILL-JOINT

FRAMES *WEATHERTIGHT*

Second—The construction is such that water which reaches
the sill joint automatically drains to the outside.

**OTHER FEATURES OF THE ANDERSEN
MASTER FRAME:**

THE INSIDE LINER—gives you, without ripping or fur-
ring, a quick way to change the jamb width of any Andersen
Master Frame. You use the same frame for wall board or plas-
ter base.

THE JAMB LUGS—with which all Master Frames are
equipped—save time and save labor cost. The jamb lugs rest
squarely on the header to give permanent support. You don't
have to block under the sill.

FIT SASH AND CUT TRIM AT THE BENCH—Andersen
Master Frames are accurately made and accurately assembled.
Builders who use Master Frames make one operation of fitting
all sash and cutting all trim at the bench. More time saved and
more labor cost saved!

The steep sill slope—the chamfered blind stop—the 5⅛
inch casings. The famous heavy duty, wearproof Andersen
pulley! These and many others are features of the quality,
labor saving construction of the Andersen Master Frame. Built
of genuine White Pine and clear Pondosa Pine—the Pondosa
frames have all important joints primed with aluminum paint.

You can do three things with Andersen Master Frames.
1—Build into the job the finest leakproof quality frame. 2—
Give lasting satisfaction to the owner. 3—Save money on every
opening.

Enclosed is a postage paid mailing card. Mail it today.
Find out all about the Andersen Master Frame. Have a demonstration. See it—and judge for yourself.

RATION

7 Heavy cast iron pulley.
Axle machine turned wheel.
bearing of hard white
maple, permanently saturated
with a non-drying lubricant.

For BIGGER
PROFITS—be sure to
sign and mail this card

I am interested in seeing a FREE
demonstration of the new Andersen
Master Frame and its money saving
features.

Please Answer this Question
What kind of frames have
you been using?

155

products

Evolving Products: The 1930s

"What can we do better?" This was the question Fred Andersen posed during a long auto trip in 1930 with his teenage assistant, Earl Swanson. In the back of the car was a sample of the company's new Master Frame, an example of the highly successful casement windows that would become Andersen's flagship products for the next half-century. "Where are we lacking? What else should we be doing that's truly different?" Fred continued.

And thus began a conversation that would forever transform Andersen's business and shake up the building materials industry. The window frame business was changing, and the company needed reinvention before a decline began. Earl, despite his youth, had some strong ideas on the subject. He suggested that the company, by producing only window frames, was missing out on an opportunity. "Most people don't know what a window frame is. You can't advertise it to the general public because it's a nonentity - it doesn't register," Earl argued. "People don't know what we're talking about. It's just a bunch of lumber that's bundled and shipped in a boxcar."

By the end of this auto trip, Fred and Earl had developed the idea of manufacturing complete windows, packaged in the factory. But it took two years to strategize and design this new window, not to mention creating a new production line in the factory to build it.

The company decided to design the new product as a casement window, long popular in European architecture, in order to capitalize on the great weakness of steel casement windows of the time, their inherent leakiness. A properly designed and fully weather stripped wood casement window, Andersen felt, would prove very attractive to builders. Thus the Andersen Master Casement, long known as "the tightest window ever built," joined the product line in 1932 and remained there for 57 years. "Our original product was rough looking in some ways," Earl Swanson recalled. Originally the Andersen Master Casement was produced unassembled, with the vertical and horizontal parts of the frame, the glazed sash, and the hardware shipped in separate cartons. In 1935 or 1936, the company began assembling the window in the factory.

Andersen put together the biggest marketing effort in its history to date to introduce the Master Casement. Mailers, special reports, and personal letters went out to the company's customers, and Andersen organized countless meetings, demonstrations, and displays. At first the results were dismal. In 1933, a year in which Andersen had hoped to rack up $2 million in sales, the Great Depression limited the gross to just $300,000. But eventually, as the country recovered economically, sales picked up. One notable sale was made to a sanatorium in Montana, which wanted the biggest window Andersen had ever produced — a window 19 units wide and requiring division into three sections for boxcar shipment.

Andersen's development of complete window units forced other companies that previously manufactured only window sash to bring out their own full window units. Few succeeded in the business.

"I lost my interest in making window and door frames about in 1935 or 1936," remembered Earl Swanson. "I became completely oriented to the complete window unit, and I knew that was the way we had to go, and I knew that our window frame business was doomed. It was just a question of when, and when we would have the courage to say, 'Look, we're going to quit doing that and concentrate and specialize on the complete window unit business.' It was a tough decision. A lot of argument. We abandoned our principal business." The company changed its name from Andersen Frame Company to Andersen Corporation in 1937, letting the world know of this transformation. The change was complete by 1951, when the last window frames rolled out of the plant.

1-3. 1935 Andersen Catalogues
By the 1930s, the Andersen catalogue had evolved into a thick, spiral-bound listing of hundreds of different window models and their accompanying hardware.

Different and Better

A "Leakproof" Window
"The sash of the Andersen Casement window was designed like a refrigerator door, with three points of contact with the frame," says Harold Meissner, Andersen's president

through much of the 1980s. In addition, the window came with phosphor bronze weatherstripping, which in laboratory testing reduced air leakage by 86 percent. Never before had a casement window been built so tightly.

Evolving Products: Into the 1940s

The **1930s** and '**40s** were the first decades in which Andersen manufactured factory-built windows. These earliest models included many of the features that would remain Andersen trademarks for years to come: innovative design, weather-tight qualities, good looks, and high-quality craftsmanship.

The Andersen Basement Window, introduced in **1934**, was the company's second product made as a complete unit and its first to be completely assembled in the factory. Its popularity owed to its weather tightness, and its resistance to rust and corrosion. It later became the first Andersen window to feature a PVC weather strip — a piece of hardware manufactured by Andersen's longtime supplier, Crane Plastics of Columbus, Ohio.

In **1938**, Andersen introduced its Narroline window, a sleekly designed double-hung product that from the start was assembled in the factory. About 90 percent of all windows installed at that time in the U. S. were double-hung, ensuring a healthy market for the window. The Narroline boasted unusually slender lines due to its narrow stiles and rails — half the width of those on traditional double-hung windows — and it eventually exceeded the Master Casement in sales. The window was also tight. Customers in Moorhead, Minn., reported in **1940** coming home after a severe dust storm had soiled the furniture and floors of the neighboring homes. Furnished with Narroline units, the customers' own

home "was just as clean as when they left it," the *Frame Maker* reported.

Still in his 20s, Earl Swanson achieved the seemingly impossible: He created a completely new kind of commercially made window, a design that enjoyed many benefits over traditional casement or double-hung windows. He called it the Horizontal Sliding Window, although the name was later changed to the Horizontal Gliding Window. "A horizontal sliding window has a great advantage over a vertically sliding window because it is not necessary to supply counter balancing means to overcome the force of gravity in order to keep the sash in an open position," Swanson wrote in a **1935** letter outlining his concept. In addition, the horizontal window design allowed for windows with much larger panes and sash than had been previously possible. "A casement that swings out and gets exposed to the winds is a hazard when you get it too big, so the concept of the original horizontal gliding window was to use large panes without that hazard," Swanson said. Andersen brought out the Horizontal Glider in **1940**. Refined over years of development and testing, it ran on a maple (later plastic) track and required only

Different and Better

The Glide

The Andersen Horizontal Gliding Window led to the company's development of the first wood sliding door in the early **1960s**. Today, the popular Andersen 200 Series Glider is helping to strengthen the company's presence in southern and western U.S. areas, where sliding windows are popular.

1. A Variety of Product Brochures

2. Basement Window Production
Production of the company's
first factory-assembled model,
shown here in 1972, remained
strong for decades.

2820¹⁵⁹

one hand for opening. The sash lifted out easily for cleaning, and the moving and fixed panes closed in a single plane for greater weather tightness.

Using the slogan, "So Simple It's Unbelievable — So Modern It's Revolutionary!", the company gave the Horizontal Glider the biggest promotional launch in its history, and the initial interest from architects and builders was intense. "During the past ten years that I have been attending conventions in different sections of the country, I do not know of a year when we have had as much interest as did our Horizontal Sliding Window," sales manager Jim Rowland wrote in the *Frame Maker* in **1940**. Alcatraz Penitentiary made a high-profile purchase of Horizontal Gliders early on — presumably for offices, not for cells. Despite its innovation, however, the Horizontal Glider was not the kind of window that builders, architects, and homeowners wanted in large quantities. It never achieved the breakthrough success that the company had expected. Although Andersen continued manufacturing the window until **1971**, World War II and the company's wartime abandonment of its product line stalled the window's introduction, and sales never met the product's potential.

The Victory Window set the standard for the conservation of in-demand materials during World War II. (See page 30 for more about this conservation-minded product.)

Featuring a pressure strip conceived by Andersen serviceman Harold Smotherman and designed in the experimental shop in Andersen's office basement, the Pressure Seal Window replaced the company's first Narroline and was supposed to go into production in **1946** when housing construction was reawakened following World War II. The scarcity of aluminum, however, delayed the Pressure Seal's introduction for three years. It used no weights, pulleys or counterbalancing equipment.

Most importantly, the Pressure Seal was perhaps the first window designed with removable sash for easy cleaning. While some competitors seized upon this innovation as a standard feature in double-hung windows, Andersen was slow to build upon it. Andersen showed little interest in the huge sales that a strongly innovative double-hung window could produce, and for years customers identified the company with casement windows. That situation would not change for years until the introduction of Andersen's Tilt-Wash windows in **1993**.

Dear Pat,
What a wonderful surprise to have the
house photo and your lovely note waiting for
us in the mailbox! I had a coffee for Drexel
Avenue neighbors last — I showed them
the picture and intere
When we moved in
we got a bid from Re
Needless to say, we will
extraordinarily beaut
I am sorry to
again. In the mean
your thoughtfulness

12/11/00

Pat Beuli
Photographer and Archivist
Anderson Corporation
100 Fourth Avenue North
Bayport, MN 55203

161

1-2. Story of a House
Built in 1933 using Andersen
Master Casement windows, a
home on Drexel Avenue in Edina,
Minnesota, and its windows
remain intact today. During the
1970s, Andersen advertising
featured this house and its long-
lasting windows.

3. Owner's Letter
Owners of the home wrote a
letter to the company in 2000.

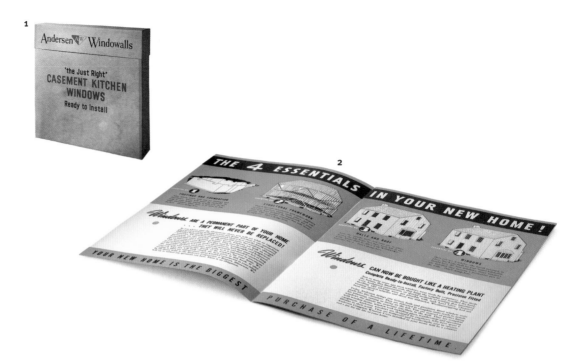

162

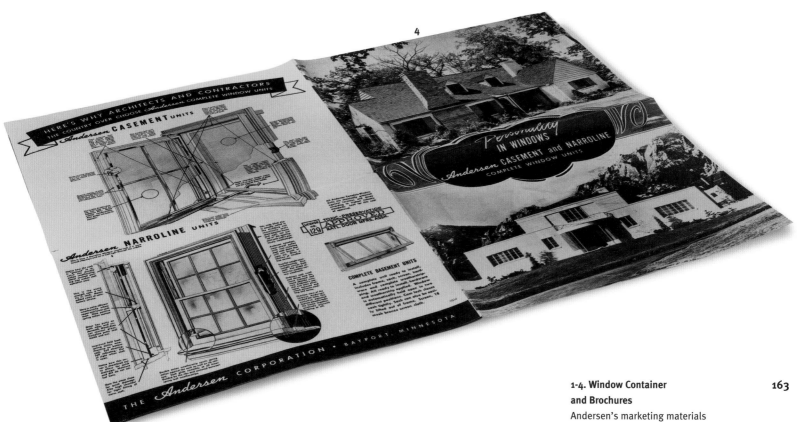

4

**1-4. Window Container
and Brochures**
Andersen's marketing materials
of the 1940s appealed to a
mix of homeowners, builders,
and architects. The phrase
"Only the Rich Can Afford Poor
Windows," which appeared
in many brochures over the
years, was popularized by Fred
Andersen, who first used it
in a speech.

163

Evolving Products: The 1950s

During the 1950s, Andersen's product line reflected the needs of families taking part in the booming suburban housing market of that decade. The one-story ranch house was in vogue, and homeowners wanted windows that were easier to use and maintain and more compatible with the architectural styles of suburban homes. Homebuilders wanted windows that could be installed with greater efficiency. In design terms, the entire decade seemed to be about stream-lining products and making things look thin. Awning windows were the answer. Andersen introduced models that became icons of mid-century America.

Perhaps the best known of Andersen's window-icons was the Flexivent, in production from 1952 through 1979. An awning window that could be mounted to open in, out, horizontally, or vertically, it offered a degree of versatility, economy, and space conservation that delighted architects and owners of new homes. The Flexivent helped Andersen nearly double its workforce and its share of the national window market within two years of its introduction. By 1954 Andersen was annually selling more than 1 million Flexivent units, igniting the development of new manufacturing processes within the company. For years the Flexivent symbolized American residen-tial life with its unique, contemporary styling as much as the Chevy in the driveway.

The Beauty-Line Window improved on the Flexivent, adding trimmer lines and, within a single frame, the combination of an awning window and a fixed upper sash giving the appearance of a double hung. Some of the earliest off the production line went to the Ladd and Elison air force bases in Alaska, where they replaced steel windows that in the severe cold frosted so heavily they admitted no light. It remained in production from 1957 to 1979.

Strutwall panels, introduced in 1959, were a concept ahead of their time. They featured a Beauty-Line Window installed in a complete wall panel. For homebuilders, Strutwall panels eliminated most of the steps involved in framing and installing windows. The Strutwall was fast, efficient and worked well in building standardized homes. A few builders loved the product, but it proved ahead of its time in an industry that was in many ways still used to hand crafting houses. Sales totals were disappointing and Strutwall stayed in production for only six years.

Different and Better

Welded Insulating Glass
For four years beginning in 1948, Andersen worked with Pittsburgh Plate Glass in pioneering the successful use of welded glass. Experiments showed that double panes of glass had superior insulating qualities. The inconvenient and and hard-to-clean storm window was suddenly obsolete. In 1952, Andersen became the first manufac-turer to offer windows with welded insulating glass. Andersen's dedication to improving the glass it used continued with the develop-ment of High-Performance glass in the 1980s.

1. Beauty-Line Window
A combination of an awning window and a fixed sash within one frame.

2. Flexivent Window
An American design icon of the 1950s and '60s.

HANDLE WITH CARE
GLASS
STAND ON EDGE

Andersen
Windowalls
FLEXIVENT *WINDOW*
✳ TRADE MARK
422

MANUFACTURED BY
ANDERSEN CORPORATION
BAYPORT · MINNESOTA

APPROVED

2

3

1

As featured in LIVING For Young Homemakers
Can you afford a part-time home?
FOUR COLORS, the name of this beach house at Westhampton, Long Island, was set by the bold panels which, from the ocean, give the effect of a painting rising out of the dune. These panels, tempered hardboard except for ...door, were designed to work well with Andersen Flexivent window units and standard ...rs. ...izer Paints ...used throughout

4

5

167

1. Flexivent Window Ad
Andersen's advertising for
the popular Flexivent window,
a residential icon of the mid-20th
century, sometimes connected
the window with leisure time
and good living.

**2-5. Beauty-Line Window
Installation**
A building crew of the 1960s
installs Beauty-Line windows
in a new house.

Arvid Wellman

Arvid Wellman, who was born in Oak Park Heights, Minnesota, knew the smells and sounds of Andersen's Bayport plant from a young age. His father worked in the factory for 33 years making mouldings and bundling frames. One day in the 1920s, the elder Wellman came home from work with some news. "He was proud to tell me he got a raise to 60 cents an hour. 'You realize that's one cent every minute,' he told me," Arvid recalls. Arvid knows the satisfaction of earning money from hard work, and as only the fourth person ever to chair the company's board he presided over some of Andersen's richest years of sales and profits.

In 1935, on summer vacation from high school, Arvid began temporary work at Andersen, manning the wood conveyor in the Cutting Department. Two years later Arvid worked his first day as a permanent Andersen employee, taking a job as a clerk in the foundry. He would spend another half-century with Andersen, working his way into the company's leadership from deep within its working ranks.

He moved from the foundry to Andersen's main office in 1940 and then worked in the billing department until going into military service in the spring of 1942. Arvid's three-and-a-half-year stint in the U.S. Army was his only break from Andersen service, but what a break it was. After 14 months at

Fort Knox, Kentucky, he requested more active service and went to England as part of an armored group. While fighting in Belgium during the Battle of the Bulge, he was captured by German forces and spent three months as a prisoner of war.

When Arvid returned to Andersen in November 1945, he began the steady progression of jobs with increasing responsibility that led to his ascension to chair. From the Scheduling Department he moved to Time Study, and then to supervisory positions in the Cutting Department. In 1960 he assumed the responsibilities of Production Manager and was also elected to the Board of Directors. Ten years later Arvid became vice president of operations. In 1976 he was named President and Chief Executive Officer. His board chairmanship began in 1981 and ended in 1992.

The Wellman years are notable for the strong sales growth Andersen experienced and for its skillful exploitation of Perma-Shield technology. He is most proud of the lasting relationships the company built during his tenure. "We respected our jobbers and suppliers," says Arvid, who remains active as chair of the Andersen Foundation. "We couldn't have been successful without successful people helping us."

168

169

products

1

Evolving Products: The 1960s, 1970s, and 1980s

In the **1930s**, Andersen Corporation reinvented itself, changing from a maker of window frames to a manufacturer of fully assembled windows. Thirty years later, new technology, several visionary thinkers, and changes in the building materials industry all conspired to produce another reinvention of Andersen.

In the space of several years, Andersen transformed from a manufacturer of all-wood windows and doors to a pioneer in the design and creation of composite products. During the **1960s**, the company staked its success on the viability of windows and doors made from a combination of wood and plastics. The line of products that ushered Andersen into this new era was Perma-Shield.

The millions of wood frames, windows, and patio doors that Andersen manufactured in its first 60 years were all remarkably good products, the best of their kind. They demanded only one thing from their owners: exterior painting. All over the country, other window manufacturers were producing products made from nearly maintenance-free materials: steel, primed wood, and aluminum. Andersen felt itself vulnerable to this new competition. So starting in the **1950s**, the company embarked upon a long effort to rid customers of even that occasional form of maintenance. The Andersen window of the future, company president Fred Andersen decided, would be a product that needed no exterior maintenance, yet would still be beautiful,

long-lasting, and energy efficient — qualities that many of the competitors' products lacked.

The quest for this maintenance-free window quickly led Andersen's research engineers in the **1950s** to plastics and a relatively new material called vinyl, which was not yet being commercially used in the building industry.

"To begin with," remembered Andersen researcher Ken Peterson, "we knew so little about vinyl that we had to look up how to spell it in the dictionary." Teaming with researchers from B.F. Goodrich Chemical Company (now PolyOne), a vinyl manufacturer, workers designed the nation's first windows constructed from hollow polyvinylchloride (PVC) frames. PVC had previously served virtually no purpose as even a component, let alone a primary material in building products. The unstable windows performed poorly, bowing easily and excessively expanding and contracting with changes in temperature. Researchers tried filling the core with sawdust, but the results were still not good enough. Then workers stuffed a core of wood into a vinyl casing, and it tested out fine, even performing well in trial installations. "But there was no practical way to accomplish this stuffing procedure on a production line basis," recalled Clare Stout, who headed Andersen's research division at the time.

There the matter rested until the early **1960s**, when Andersen president Earl Swanson sent John Kohl, a newly hired and multilingual expert in

170

vinyls and plastics, to Europe to see what he could learn from the plastics industry there. In West Germany Kohl heard of an impressive new manufacturing process that permitted the manufacture of vinyl-over-wood window shutters. The Italian inventor Luigi Zanini had developed a concept that made it possible to extrude a layer of PVC over a wood base. Kohl rushed to Zanini's plant, saw the dies and the machinery, and negotiated an option on the vinyl extrusion process that gave Andersen time to decide whether to become the sole American licensee.

The company jumped on the opportunity, and in 1963 it produced its first test windows. But making rigid vinyl windows required much more than setting up some new equipment. For three years, Andersen tested the process, adapted new equipment and conducted more research. Kohl, who traveled to Europe 38 times during this period, developed a new vacuum-forming method of applying the vinyl, and Ken Peterson, building a new machine in the Andersen shop, discovered a way to simultaneously "weld" the vinyl corners of the window sash for weather-tightness that is still used today. Other Andersen employees designed and built hoppers, stands, calibrator blocks, and a system to cool the hot vinyl. Designing a new machine could take six months. Sometimes, as in any experimental work, there were mishaps. "The first time we were reheating the vinyl, the extruder made a hot pocket of plastic," says Dale Carmichael, who maintained machines involved in the new process. "It burned and produced a gas. There was a puff of smoke in the room, and we had to clear the area. These were a lot different from the machines in the rest of the plant. And there were no schools we could attend in order to learn how to use them."

All this work took place in a locked area of the plant, off-limits to most employees. A green plywood wall separated the vinyl work from Andersen's ongoing production. "There were rumors of a new type of window, but we really didn't know what was going on," says Eugene "Peanuts" Bell, a long time Andersen employee.

When they finally saw the sort of new product Andersen was developing, some employees were not comfortable. The company was full of workers dedicated to wood craftsmanship, and some believed that plastic — with its connotations of cheapness and breakability — was "un-Andersen." They didn't see the beauty of vinyl, and many disliked the pungent smell of the vinyl extruders, which was nothing like the smell of working with wood. Only time allowed everyone to adjust to this new material.

171

1. Perma-Shield Production
Andersen quickly became a leader in the manufacture of windows made from composite materials.

2. Perma-Shield Brochure
The company's early Perma-Shield literature took on the task of introducing a completely new kind of window to customers.

The effort to create Perma-Shield windows, as the new product would be called, and the reinvention of Andersen into a maker of composite products, not only required the most massive investment of money, time, and brainpower in Andersen's history. It also involved great risk. "The corporation was then primarily known as a wood window company," says Jack Piepel, who spent decades in research and product development. "There was no separate organization within Andersen for Perma-Shield. Some customers weren't sure about it, and they waited a year or more before trying it. But eventually everyone accepted it and it became highly successful, establishing for the industry a completely new building products category: clad windows and doors. The advantage we had was that our people understood that materials and processes had to be integrated into a successful design to make a product that would perform. There was so much testing and study. We had to be convinced that the product would perform over the life of a building."

Once real production began in 1966, a greatly altered Andersen plant was working around the clock. Some of the extruder operators worked 12-hour shifts, seven days a week, handling hot vinyl that often exceeded 350 degrees. "We threw ourselves into it, got involved, and helped the company tremendously," says Carl Sandberg, Andersen's first vinyl production worker.

Andersen initially envisioned Perma-Shield products for commercial customers, but the demand was greatest among home owners and builders. As production grew more efficient, the price per unit dropped lower than the price for some all-wood windows. Soon Andersen had Perma-Shield casements, Narroline double-hung models, gliding doors, and awning windows. (The line was called Perma-Sheath in Canada.) By 1969, the incredible had happened — the Perma-Shield line accounted for half of Andersen's business. The company's reinvention had succeeded. The company built its last primed wood products around 1990. (Not until the 1980s, when the popularity of Andersen's "crank-out" casement windows began to wane, would the company grow due for yet another reinvention.)

Perma-Shield had launched not only a new Andersen Corporation, but also a revolutionary new segment of the building materials industry. Composites — the combination of wood, plastics, and other materials — would eventually dominate the industry. Composites would also play an important role in Andersen's next reinvention during the 1990s.

1. Perma-Shield Brochure
This literature from around 1970 focuses on the benefits for commercial building owners of windows made from composite materials.

2. New Equipment
The company's reinvention as a user of composite materials in the 1960s required the retooling of the Andersen plant and the development of new equipment.

172

Different and Better

Research and Testing

Problems with the durability of Perma-Shield products that surfaced in the late **1970s** and early **1980s** set Andersen on a course of product research and testing that paid big dividends in the years to come but not without pain and cost to Andersen. Andersen began working with Aspen Research Corporation in the late '80s, a partnership that produced new methods to test products in artificial and natural environments for their ability to withstand extremes in temperature and humidity. One result was a solution for PVC cracking and peeling problems that had affected some early Perma-Shield products and prompted many service requests. The partnership with Aspen also produced Fibrex material, Andersen's most promising composite material of the 21st century. Aspen Research is now an Andersen subsidiary.

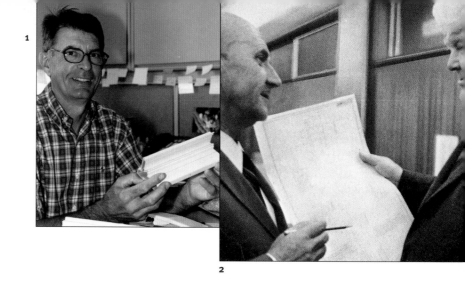

1

2

3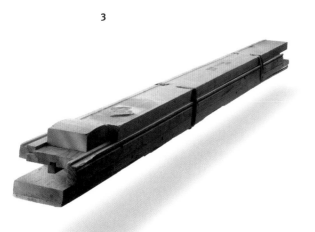

4

5

6 →

174

Men of Vinyl

Andersen people have not forgotten Luigi Zanini, the inventor of the process that allowed Andersen to start making Perma-Shield windows.

A two-story brick building served as his business headquarters, and his family lived on the top floor. "He was a typical Italian inventor," remembers Joe Puppin, who served as Zanini's chief assistant before coming to work at Andersen in 1968. "He was a bit moody, not very interested in the details of production, which he always said would have to be figured out." And he loved racing motorcycles.

Zanini visited Bayport a dozen times to help Andersen set up Perma-Shield production. He was not fluent in English at the time, sometimes leaving Andersen employees puzzled about his instructions. "I remember him shouting, 'Left! Left! More air!'" says Carl Sandberg.

Zanini's bond with the company led to the hiring of Puppin, who has spent most of his Andersen career developing extrusion process tools for Perma-Shield and Fibrex material products and holds several patents. "I was 25 years old and could not speak English when I first came," he says. "But that did not stop people from inviting me to their homes. The Andersen people were friendly, and they gave me an opportunity to work and advance. I've never regretted my move here — Andersen is the best company I've ever encountered."

1. Joe Puppin
Puppin, once Luigi Zanini's chief assistant, became one of Andersen's most valuable assets in the transition to the manufacture of composite windows and doors.

2. Perma-Shield Partners
Luigi Zanini (left) and John Kohl confer during the early stages of Perma-Shield production.

3-5. Evolution of the Window Joint
After leading the industry with the production of the Locked Sill-Joint, Andersen again set new technological standards with the development of Perma-Shield and, in the 1990s, windows made of Fibrex material.

6. Luigi Zanini
The Italian inventor, an important Andersen partner, impressed employees with his brilliance and love of motorcycles.

Evolving Products: The 1990s and the Early 21st Century

By the mid-1990s, Andersen was deep in a decade-long decline in market share with the added problems of channel disloyalty and increased competitiveness from makers of mid-price products. The company's premium customers were drifting away. Andersen clearly had to change its way of doing business. For the company to survive, it had to consolidate its channel and implement a program to rebuild dealer loyalty, make it easier for builders and dealers to deal with Andersen, move from dependence on made-to-stock manufacturing, and learn just-in-time manufacturing of make-to-order products. In order to grow, Andersen had to augment its windows with doors, introduce mid-band and high-end premium products and price categories, build business in the western and southern U.S., court replacement window customers, and offer all customers more value.

The sleeping giant awakened, inspired by Jerry Wulf in 1995 with Andersen's first strategic plan and by Don Garofalo as the plan was revised in 1997-98 and implemented through 2003. In its centennial year, Andersen is again growing. Strong, confident, hard working, strategic and determined, the company has aligned capability and capacity with strategies, created differentiated and sustainable strategies, and tapped the needs of its market segments to guide priorities, decisions, and accomplishments.

The result? In 1999, for the first time in a decade, Andersen gained market share from its competitors, with each of its customer segments

176

adding to the momentum. These are the products that signaled a shift in the market and produced that upsurge.

Andersen 400 Series Windows

For decades nearly every Andersen product fell into the "premium" category, intended for builders and homeowners who wanted the highest grade of materials in their windows and doors. At the close of the 1990s, that familiar line of products became the 400 Series of windows and patio doors. Appealing to small contractors and do-it-yourself homeowners, the 400 Series line features energy-efficient High Performance glass with a specialized metallic coating that slashes heating and cooling costs, a wide range of sizes, colors, and other features, including the option to order designs from the Andersen Art Glass

Different and Better

Mid-Range Pricing
By breaking out of its old practice of manufacturing only premium-priced windows and doors, Andersen in 1999 was able to gain market share for the first time in a decade. Following its 1999 five-year strategic plan, the company developed new products that won an important partnership with The Home Depot, the nation's largest home

improvement retailer. Andersen's mid-priced products have not only helped to develop new customers, but they have also displaced the products of competitors by bringing a full range of price choices, all within the Andersen brand, to the retailer's customers — making Andersen the premier millwork brand at The Home Depot.

Collection. Woodwright windows, Andersen's first custom double-hung window was added to the 400 Series in **2003**, advancing window design by including architectural features and technological enhancements that carry the tradition of the double-hung window into the new millennium. The Woodwright window gets its inspiration from history, while it provides a view squarely into the future. It brings traditional styling together with both standard and custom sizing into a single product using Fibrex material as its primary structural component — making it ideal for use as a replacement product for remodeling, in new construction, and where precise dimensions are needed.

Andersen 200 Series Windows

In **2000**, Andersen introduced the first of the 200 Series products, designed to appeal to buyers in a lower price range. Builders who earlier found Andersen products beyond their reach can now give their customers products representing all the hallmarks of the Andersen brand: craftsmanship, high quality, and beauty. The 200 Series line also plays an important role in strengthening Andersen's presence in regions of the country where sales have historically been weaker than others. The 200 Series Gliding Window, introduced in **2001**, offers a great opportunity for Andersen to make serious inroads in the southern and western U.S., the areas that account for more than 70 percent of the nation's sales of gliding windows.

1. Andersen 400 Series Door
Doors rank among the fastest growing categories of Andersen products.

2. Andersen 400 Series Windows
Andersen introduced this line in 2000.

3. Andersen 200 Series Installation
In just a few years, the new line grew into one of the most popular in North America.

Doors

For a time at the end of the 20th century, Andersen was in a downward spiral. By the **1990s**, the company had lost a third of its window sales as competitors emerged with products and pricing strategies that better met the needs of customers. The company temporarily rested on its laurels as sales slid and customers began growing dissatisfied. Andersen's researchers and designers did not receive adequate support for their work, and they divided into separate and sometimes uncommunicative camps.

In the midst of this crisis, doors emerged as a bright spot at Andersen. The company had begun marketing its first patio door, a gliding product, in **1961**. It followed with a Perma-Shield model about ten years later. But it was Andersen's first hinged patio door, the Frenchwood door, that in a sense served as the salvation of the company during dark times. Met with some internal skepticism when introduced in the late **1980s**, the Frenchwood door was a huge success. Almost alone in the Andersen product catalogue, it led the company to new customers.

Since then, as Andersen has solidly reassumed the industry's top position, doors have remained crucially important in the company's strategies for its various market segments. The acquisition of EMCO Enterprises in **2001** enabled Andersen to offer a superb line of storm and screen doors — typically an after-market purchase — through its retail partner, The Home Depot. KML, acquired a few months later, allowed the company to offer handcrafted entry doors that complemented the existing 400 and 200 Series lines and appealed to super-premium customers. Improvements in channel distribution launched by Andersen Logistics place the right doors in the hands of customers faster and more efficiently than ever before in the company's history.

As a result, Andersen's many segments of customers can now find the doors they need — exactly when and where they need them. Doors continue to lead the company's ascent into the prime phase of its business cycle.

1. A Successful Launch
The Frenchwood patio door, shown here in literature from 1999, was one of Andersen's most successful products of the 1990s.

2. EMCO Door
When EMCO Enterprises joined the Andersen family in 2001, its products and culture – similar to Andersen's in its focus on quality and strong employee partnerships – were strengths.

3. KML Door and Window
Like the aquisition of EMCO the same year, KML's combination with Andersen helped serve customers better.

Acquisitions

Andersen's careful series of acquisitions begun in the **1990s** is an important part of the company's plan. Dashwood Industries Limited joined the Andersen family in **1995**, adding roof windows to the product assortment. (Another **1995** acquisition, R. LaFlamme & Friere Inc. of Quebec, makers of all-vinyl products, proved incompatible with Andersen's business and was sold three years later.) The **2001** purchase of EMCO Enterprises, Inc., an Iowa-based maker of high-quality and innovative storm doors, strengthened Andersen's position with do-it-yourself homeowners and small homebuilders. Ontario, Canada-based KML Windows Inc., which joined the Andersen family later that same year, added a doubly potent diversification of the product line: a line of doors and windows that both complemented Andersen's existing 400 Series line and appealed to customers interested in super-premium products. With the acquisition of each company, Andersen gained marketing, sales, and order-fulfillment strengths that benefit all of Andersen Corporation.

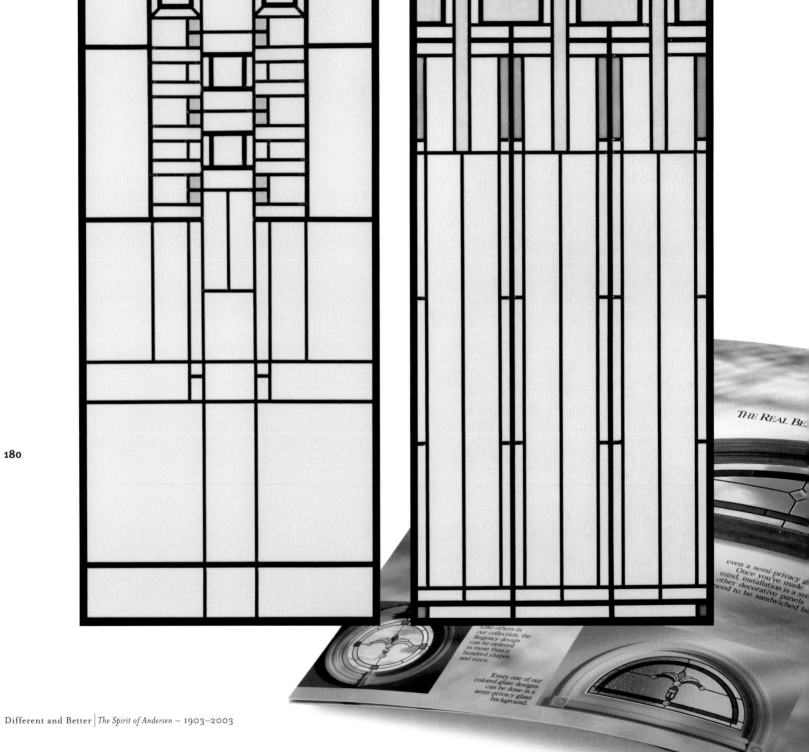

3

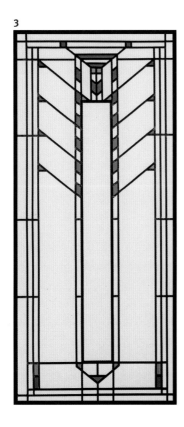

4

5

1–5 Art Glass Windows and Brochure
These Frank Lloyd Wright designs, as
well as other styles in the brochure,
offer many choices to buyers of
Andersen's 400 Series windows.

products

Fibrex Material

In 1991, facing rising lumber costs, Andersen teamed with Aspen Research to develop a building material that could replace wood in a variety of applications. The result was a new vinyl-based product that, like Perma-Shield in the 1960s, would mark a great advance in the development of composite materials. It was called Fibrex material. "If you take 60 percent vinyl and 40 percent reclaimed wood fibers, and mix them together using our patented process, you get one variation of Fibrex," says Don Garofalo, Andersen's CEO. Durable and usable for many purposes, Fibrex has a low thermal expansion rate, is virtually resistant to rotting, insulates well, and retains its rigidity in temperatures as high as 203 degrees.

Those qualities lend themselves to a wealth of applications, and Andersen has spent years experimenting with innovative uses for Fibrex. In the company's own product line, Fibrex first appeared in the subsill of the Frenchwood hinged patio door. Fibrex has played a crucial role in the dramatic success of Renewal by Andersen, serving as an important component of the company's line of custom-made, architecturally authentic replacement windows. Fibrex is also a key ingredient in the 400 Series Double Hung window.

The origins of Fibrex actually go back to the early 1970s, when Andersen experimentally blended wood fibers and other materials with polyvinylchloride. Samples of the new material were painted and set outdoors for weathering. The results were good, but nobody knew how to use this new material. It took the passage of nearly 20 years, and the advent of more efficient machinery, to produce Fibrex, which has greater stiffness than the earlier material. "It's often the case that new technologies and incentives in the market allow for the resurrection of old experiments," says Jack Piepel, retired vice president of engineering, who took part in Fibrex's early development. Now Andersen's challenge is to use the environmental friendliness, insulation value in hot or cold, and easy maintenance of Fibrex to strengthen the demand for this product of new technology. In the future, the company will license Fibrex technology to other non-competing manufacturers, bringing this new material in a multitude of forms to homes and businesses around the world.

Different and Better

Composite Materials

Ever since introducing the vinyl-clad Perma-Shield line in 1966, Andersen has been a leader in developing composite materials for doors and windows. "Composite materials simply offer new functionality," says Kurt Heikkila, senior vice president of Advanced Technology. "The integrity of the composite material is better than it is for the individual ingredients that go into it. Fibrex material, for instance, offers better energy efficiency than wood, better thermal performance, and the ability to produce customized sizes more readily."

1. Fibrex Pellets
Made from vinyl and wood fibers,
Fibrex is superior to pure wood
in many respects.

The Importance of Research

In the early **1930s**, when Andersen launched its first efforts to design advanced frames and windows, the research and technology department (then called Design Engineering) came into its own. Headed by Earl Swanson, Dick Wilmes, and Vern Fredrickson, this beginning research and development unit devoted itself to the search for "different and better," subjecting Andersen products to a variety of primitive tests. Adjacent to the boiler room, in a nondescript shed, workers cooked up reproductions of some of nature's worst scenarios — dust storms, downpours of rain, and floods.

Design and testing remain vitally important functions in the development of Andersen products. Long wind tunnels able to kick up hurricane-force gales, heat and cold chambers capable of mimicking the conditions of the polar caps and the desert, and devices that can produce extremes of dry and wet are part of the testing regimen for new products. Windows, hardware, finishes, and packaging materials all undergo testing.

Research and product design progressed rapidly during the **1950s** and **'60s**, when a building boom and the advent of vinyl-clad products demanded a constant stream of innovations. Vern Frederickson headed the team that developed the Flexivent window and other models, and John Kohl was responsible for many of the new ideas that made the Perma-Shield line possible.

For a time in the final quarter of the 20th century, however, Andersen did not emphasize the development of new products — the innovative, brilliantly designed windows and doors that the company vitally needs in order to sustain its leadership in the industry.

Fortunately, research and development is now enthusiastically supported at Andersen, as it was for most of the company's first 100 years. A strategic research plan directs the whole company. In **1997** Andersen acquired Aspen Research Corporation, the firm with which it developed Fibrex material. At the time, the company changed its focus from the manufacturing of products to identifying and meeting the needs of select categories of customers. Aspen's expertise and knowledge of Andersen's markets has enabled the company to launch unprecedented numbers of new products in recent years, including mid-priced windows, grille options, sidelights and transoms. Research at Andersen now propels the company toward a target, rather than shooting in all directions — and the company is once again gaining market share as customers embrace Andersen's solutions.

184

185

1. Instron Testing
Products undergo thorough
testing of their strength
and durability.

2. Artificial Sunlight
High-tech testing equipment
mimics years of sunlight
exposure.

3. Researchers at Work
Research Department members
(clockwise from bottom)
Lyle Ward, Rod Swanson,
Dick Wilmes, Lawton Porter, and
Vern Fredricksen examine a
window, circa 1960.

products

Jerry Wulf

Jerry Wulf, who served as Andersen's president and CEO throughout much of the 1990s, came into the office as an energetic executive. This quality served him well as he took over the company from the leaders of an earlier generation and prepared Andersen for the changes that would return the company to a strong footing. Andersen Corporation became stronger, more progressive, and better attuned to its traditions during his tenure.

After earning a degree in architecture and ending a four-year stint in the Navy, Jerry joined Andersen in 1959 as a sales and service trainee. Following several years in Pennsylvania, Jerry returned to Bayport as a sales training manager. "That's when I came to understand what a wonderful company Andersen was," Jerry says. "I never had the feeling that I was lost in it. People knew and helped me."

In 1970, Jerry was named director of research and development. "Perma-Shield was already under our belt. Adding permanent color to the vinyl was the new focus, and we produced Terratone." In addition, the energy crisis of the '80s helped push Andersen in new directions of research. The result was the invention of energy efficient glass used in Andersen products starting in the early '80s. Low-emmisivity glass, or High-Performance glass, uses coatings on the glass to reflect heat back outdoors during hot, summer months and allows radiant heat from the sun to enter and warm interiors during the cold winter season.

By the end of the 1980s, Jerry was beginning to think about early retirement. An unexpected phone call dashed those plans. "Arvid Wellman, the CEO, called," Jerry recalls. "He asked if I would be willing to be nominated for president. I was speechless." Not too speechless to accept the position in 1990, however, and Jerry also assumed the role of CEO in 1992.

Despite its unquestionable strengths, Andersen presented Jerry with difficult decisions. For several years market share had been declining. Andersen needed new ways of doing business. Soon Jerry established an executive committee to strengthen business planning and management, and together with the committee he developed the company's first strategic plan to reverse the trend. Though he took a conservative approach to business, he presided over the launch of Renewal by Andersen. Renewal's business model — focusing on retail sales of made-to-order products made from Fibrex composite material and installed in homes — was completely new for Andersen.

Another big change began with the decision that the two-step distribution channel was outdated and not contributing to Andersen's success. Eighty years earlier, Fred Andersen had established wholesale distribution as the means of bringing Andersen products to market. "But eventually that set-up became restrictive," Jerry says.

Highly regarded by his peers and coworkers, Jerry retired in 1998 and has continued as a member of the Andersen Foundation board.

186

Renewal by Andersen

Renewal by Andersen was launched in **1995** after several years in which Andersen's leadership hotly debated its merits. It was one thing to manufacture windows, some argued, but quite another thing to make a retail business out of replacing old windows and installing new ones. But when viewed through the lens of the company's strategic plan, including Andersen's commitment to better serving the growing "do-it-for-me" segment of the market, the potential of Renewal by Andersen grew clear.

Renewal by Andersen was first discussed in **1992**, when Kurt Heikkila, then with Aspen Research Corporation, and Don Garofalo talked about possible uses for Fibrex material, the company's new composite compound. "We thought about working with a new customer, the consumer," Kurt recalls. "If we were going to be retailers, we wanted to have a good relationship with consumers — we wouldn't call them if they hadn't called us, and we would do the whole job and make it a great experience. We realized this was the way to go from our relationships with our other customers. Then we visited Europe and saw that nearly all of the windows there are old and need replacement at some point. We wanted to do it in an architecturally authentic way, and to make it a real Andersen experience."

Replacing windows in a manner consistent with the "Andersen experience" revolutionized the business. Research showed that many companies that provided home improvement and replacement

services had a negative reputation for high pressure sales tactics and scams. "What we found was that people didn't necessarily want a better window, they wanted a better experience," Don Garofalo says. And, by customers' accounts, they have received a better experience from Renewal by Andersen. One customer called the crew that arrived "punctual, courteous, polite, efficient, and professional. They listened to us, asking the right questions." Another customer echoed that appraisal, adding, "I congratulate you on what appears to me a very special company that is not settling for 'just the norm' in attitude, work, and follow-through."

"We are fortunate that Don and his team had the vision to imagine the kind of company Renewal by Andersen would be and the practices it would use," says Craig Evanich, Renewal's president. Renewal by Andersen has rapidly become a major player in the replacement-market segment by adhering to these principles:
— No telemarketing. Renewal is not the kind of company that makes sales calls to customers at home just as they're sitting down to dinner.
— No pressure. During free, at-home visits, Renewal representatives discuss with customers their specific needs, show samples, take measurements, and offer a written estimate that's guaranteed for 30 days. "What we won't do is pressure you to make a purchase before you're ready," Craig says.

1-2. Renewal by Andersen
This innovative enterprise is a
retail operation that retrofits
older homes with architecturally
accurate new windows.

— Courtesy and efficiency. Installers show up at the scheduled time, remove old windows, dispose of them properly, install new windows, and clean up after themselves. "Having retired from the trade some years ago, I have very high standards for workmanship, especially in my own home," one customer wrote. "Your staff was terrific. They showed up on time, did quality work, and most importantly, met my personal standards for a job well done."

The division opened its first retail store in 1995. Now headquartered in Cottage Grove, Minnesota, Renewal by Andersen is one of the fastest growing parts of Andersen Corporation. Part of that success is due to Renewal's set of values, which include a strong customer focus, safety, high integrity, innovation, teamwork, and corporate citizenship. "We have definitely benefited from being part of the Andersen brand, which assures customers that they can trust us, that they will be treated well, and that we stand behind our product," says Craig. Customers have responded by praising Renewal as painless, convenient, and minimally disruptive. Its custom-produced windows, made to the exact size and architectural specifications of the customer, are the most significant use so far of Fibrex material, which offers unusual manufacturing flexibility and significant energy savings for customers. In addition, the windows use low emissivity double-pane glass, adding even more energy efficiency.

The results speak for themselves. With company-owned operations in five U.S. cities and 50 affiliates representing it in territories nationwide, Renewal is experiencing double-digit growth. The customers know why. "I had eleven windows installed in my home, and I am writing to tell you how extremely happy I am with them," declared one. "I am telling everyone I can about the wonderful service I received! This has been the largest project I've done on my house so far, and your staff made it completely painless. Thank you very much."

Potentially a billion-dollar business, Renewal "has a future dedicated to continuous improvement," Evanich says. In creating Fibrex material, Andersen is also prepared to fully exploit it. Renewal by Andersen shows that thinking in terms of "different and better" can result in innovative and successful new ways of business.

1. Headquarters
The central offices of Renewal by Andersen in Cottage Grove, Minn.

190

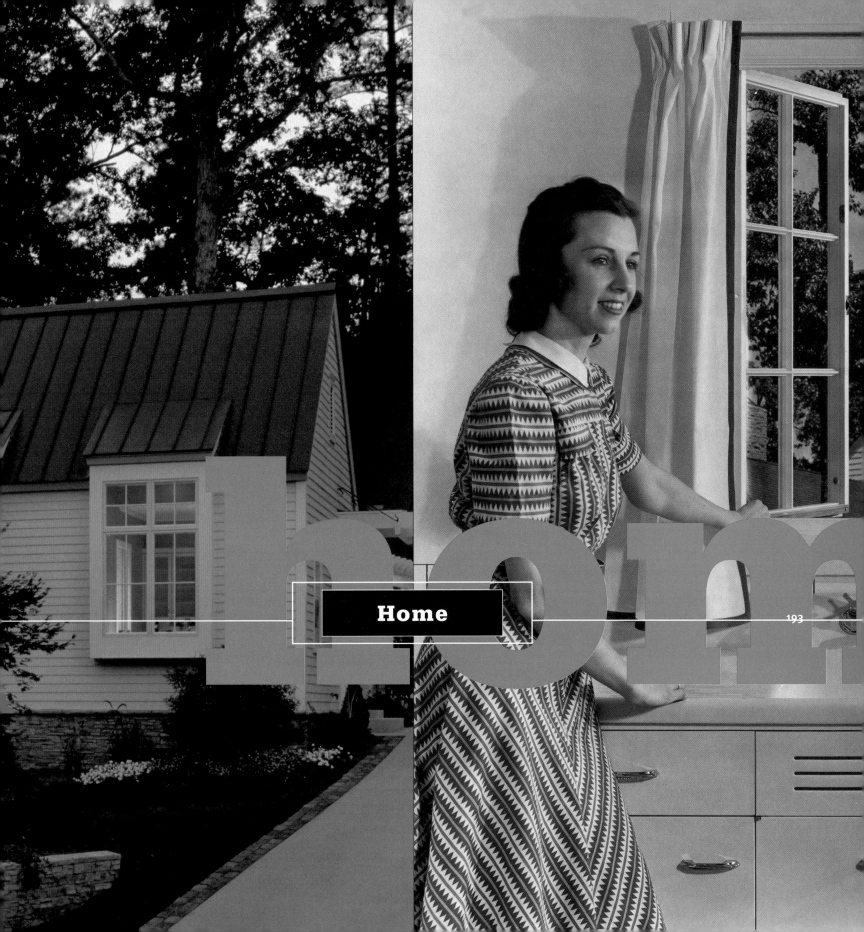

Home

"ANDERSEN IS A PERMANENT PART OF THE BEAUTY, COMFORT, AND SECURITY THAT HOMES PROVIDE."

—Phil Donaldson

194

195

home

Future

Throughout the past 100 years, two forces have had the greatest influence on the company that has evolved into Andersen Corporation. The first is innovation, and the second is the creation of a distinctive culture resilient enough to survive tumultuous change yet focused enough on excellence to keep Andersen at the top of its industry. These forces, fundamental to the company's success, are the keys to Andersen's **future**.

Don Garofalo

A visionary and long-range thinker, Don Garofalo led Andersen through a critical phase of reinvention. During his tenure as president and CEO, the company halted a steady loss of market share, while Andersen's development of new products, marketing and sales efforts, and strategic acquisitions achieved a dramatic expansion of the company's market reach. The company emerged as a flourishing enterprise with nine manufacturing sites, several new distribution centers and a new focus on serving a greater variety of customers. "I was brought in to change things, and as my wife tells me, that's been the focus of my whole career," Don explains.

A graduate of the University of Minnesota School of Architecture, Don joined Andersen in 1964. He began as a sales representative in Indiana. "The passion of the company was part of the spell cast over me," he says. A few years later, he returned to Bayport to assist Jerry Wulf in sales administration. "I focused on commercial accounts, and we took clients to two Swiss fondue dinners a week," he remembers. Around this time, Don joined four other Andersen employees in forming The Friendly Valley Boys, a band that entertained clients with original lyrics set to popular songs.

In 1969, Don moved to the Research and Development Department and served in several capacities before being named head of the department in 1990. There he developed his research background and skills in interpreting complex business conditions. Don was appointed vice president of Business Planning and Development in 1993, responsible for marketing, sales, and research and development. As senior vice president, a position he accepted in 1995, Don oversaw the successful launch of Renewal by Andersen, which took on the fast-growing window replacement market segment and made the first significant use of Fibrex material. His collaborative management style strengthened the company's ability to forge decisions and execute new plans.

Don has also championed Andersen's role as strong partner in its communities. He gave momentum to the company's support of such Twin Cities community jewels as the Courage Center, the Children's Museum, and the Science Museum of Minnesota, and he has led an expansion of the philanthropic activities of the corporation.

As president, Don worked out of a conviction that the commitment, abilities, and loyalty of Andersen employees would assure Andersen's reinvention and success. Refocusing the company on customers and markets "was like turning the Queen Mary around. But now we have institutionalized planning and a five-year plan. We have an outstanding and balanced board. Our employees are the best in the industry. And our market share is growing again," he says.

As chief executive officer and vice chair of Andersen's board, Don continues to contribute his vision, experience, and leadership skills to the company's success.

200

The Long View

Fred Andersen once said that the point of looking back at the past "is to enable us to select those practices which have contributed to our success, and to see that they are continued." Andersen Corporation and its employees now have the chance to look back upon an entire century, a span of years that have seen the company grow into North America's largest maker of windows and doors. That Andersen has reached 100 years with such a strong sense of direction means that many of its original practices still work well, the principles that customers, employees, and business partners recognize as the key elements of the Andersen brand. Andersen, as always, stands for a dedication to quality, innovation, ethical conduct, environmental stewardship, appreciation for its employees, and the comforts of home. While those principles form an important part of Andersen's business strategy, viewing them as a license to resist change will not carry the company into the years ahead.

Looking back also demands the harder task of looking forward to determine what must change. The company's shifts into the production of bundled frames, factory-assembled windows, and products made from composite materials show that Andersen has a tradition of making changes that safeguard its future. The difficult years of the 1980s and 1990s, in which Andersen's market share slipped, offered another such opportunity. During that era, changes in Andersen's world — including the emergence of customers, rather than distributors, as the dominant power in the marketplace and the appearance of a large demand for mid-price products — made some company practices, even long venerated ones, obsolete. The needs of customers had moved beyond the company's capabilities. Painfully, the company realized that it was essential for Andersen to rediscover its customers and to identify their product needs, preferred price points, and ways of doing business. In order to do so, Andersen had to take greater control of its channel of distribution, update its selling practices, and develop a wide variety of products in order to bring itself closer to customers. It had to refocus the attention of its board of directors onto long range planning. Redefining the company's target markets also became a necessity. If Andersen didn't do all that — if it held to its old identity as simply a premium window company — it would watch its competitors continue to gain ground, leaving Andersen at risk.

So the company altered course because it had to — and because adapting to changing conditions is what has allowed Andersen to thrive for a century. Every Andersen employee of the past decade has helped make the necessary changes, thus safeguarding the company's position as an industry leader and shaping its future. As in so many times in the past, leaders came forward to create a plan for success and

carry it out. Sarah Andersen, the great-granddaughter of company founders Hans and Sarah "Sadie" Andersen, guided the board of directors to a stronger advisory role in the governance of the business. Meanwhile, current CEO Don Garofalo and company President and COO Jim Humphrey have focused the company's attention on building the new Andersen.

The new Andersen first stirred in the mid-1990s. Anyone who sees the company now, with its steady gain in market share, has to be astounded by the progress. In recent years, Andersen's planning has created:

— a network of company-owned, independent and aligned distributors with over half of all volume flowing through company-owned operations;

— a wide variety of products at various price points, capturing for Andersen more business in the mid-price, premium, and super-premium market segments;

— improvements in both the company's retail capability and its make-to-order manufacturing competency through Renewal by Andersen, which is becoming a major player in the replacement window market segment;

— expansion of the company's presence in the southern and western United States, with products designed for the needs of those market areas;

— and the attainment of a new sales record — more than $2 billion — to mark Andersen's 100th year of business.

Andersen's five-year strategic plan, introduced late in 1998 and now nearly at its completion, committed Andersen to changing the way it does business. "The puzzle of how Andersen became more successful in the marketplace could not be solved one piece at a time," says Don Garofalo, "or one initiative at a time." Reinventing Andersen would not work as a stand-alone project. Only integration planning and implementation teams that linked all parts of the company would ensure success. This complex and daring undertaking required new responsibilities for executive managers and new ways of communicating Andersen's future to employees. "We know what we're doing, where we're going, and how to get there," Don says.

Today, Andersen's blueprint for the future focuses on serving five customer segments: volume home builders, custom home builders, professional remodelers, do-it-yourselfer homeowners, and do-it-for-me homeowners. An array of product lines in mid-price, premium, and super-premium categories are offered to meet the needs of each of these segments.

In Andersen's view, the future is neither distant nor hazy. Company leaders believe that Andersen's success in the 21st century will depend upon the diligence with which it investigates the continually evolving needs of its customers, along with its creativity in developing new products and materials. Materials, especially composite compounds like Fibrex material, are important. The company, for example, is banking that the applications of Fibrex material will multiply manyfold as it takes its place as a durable and commonly used building component.

Some of Andersen's most interesting explorations of the future take place in a warren of cubicles and conference rooms. In one room, sketches cover the walls of products freshly hatched from the minds of engineers, designers, and researchers. A few of these products will eventually bear the Andersen label; most will never make their way off the drawing board. Another room houses an amazing collection of working models of new windows and doors that seems plucked from a science-fiction movie.

This is the home of Andersen's Project Odyssey, where employees combine technology with environmental, social and cultural trends to define the window and door of the future. Project Odyssey, a research and development initiative that began in 1999 and has now evolved into an ongoing discovery process in the company's advanced technologies area, sees windows and doors not just as passive portals to the outside world, but as things that can interact with users. In trade shows across the country, Andersen has demonstrated products that apply existing technology in innovative ways. Windows will have invisible screens

that keep insects out, built-in audio and video systems, embedded fire alarms that direct firefighters to rooms that contain people, and integrated climate control devices. Your window can also be a clock or computer screen. Your doorframe can serve as a beautiful load-bearing support for your house. The point is to drive innovation back into the window business.

In the past, windows and doors were mainly points of contact between the outside of a building and the inside. Not so in the future. They will offer people a new kind of interface. "There's no reason why you can't run the Internet on your kitchen window, or watch television," says Phil Donaldson, Andersen's senior vice president of marketing and business development. "Over the past 100 years, the window has already changed the way people use their homes. What's new with Project Odyssey is that it lets us research how to integrate new technology into windows. It gives us the ability to invent this new interface product."

The initial results of Project Odyssey show that trying to produce something different and better often yields something truly innovative. "The product concepts we're exploring will change the way we think of ventilation and the way we use screens in our windows," Donaldson says.

From the high vantage point of a century's experience, the years ahead look bright. "In the future," says Jim Humphrey, Andersen's president and chief operating officer, "we will be our customers' best partner, their best business solution. They will judge us by how we add value to their business." In order to be the best solution, Andersen will become even more passionate than it is now about learning about what customers need and want. This passion and intensity, of course, is part of the Andersen tradition, the same tradition that made sales director Jim Rowland a nationally known and former industry figure throughout much of the last century. "The Andersen of the future will be a much larger company" Jim Humphrey adds. "We will be more of an assembly, sales, and distribution organization, one that produces new categories of products, building off the Fibrex technology as well as others."

"Andersen has only scratched the surface of the opportunity available if we find ways to better partner with our customers," Humphrey says. "Loyalty is the absence of a viable alternative." The company has shifted its direction and set its sights on its identified customers. It created new distribution channels and formulated new approaches to research and manufacturing, all to respond quickly with solutions that will best serve Andersen customers. Its strategic acquisitions of KML, EMCO, and other businesses have been designed to bring more value to specific Andersen customers. The Andersen brand,

that precious commodity that no other company possesses, has been leveraged to mean something valuable to each customer category. In the future, more than ever, others will measure Andersen by the vision of its people and the contributions that its values make to its communities — and by the dedication with which it adds value to customers. "In short, we must redefine customer satisfaction, and then earn customer loyalty — daily," says Humphrey.

Andersen's business model has changed, just as it has several other times in the past 100 years, but not its principles or conduct as a company. "Andersen still thinks of itself as a family, although a much bigger one than in the past," says Don Garofalo. "But the family ethic is still strong, and with that comes a strong commitment to the people who make our company successful. Our vision calls for balanced growth, and our employees are the key for that growth to happen. How they work — how this company conducts its business — will be the sole reason for our future success."

In its centennial year, customers are once again drawn to Andersen and feel an uncommon trust that the company is again working for their success. "What a gift," observes Don Garofalo. It's a gift that will sustain Andersen Corporation long into the future.

Jim Humphrey

Jim Humphrey became Andersen's president and COO in December **2002** with a clear idea of what the company represents. "Andersen stands for innovative solutions, a trusted brand, and integrity," he says. "Although we can change the policies and practices of Andersen, we cannot change the core principles and values. They are how we are known among our employees and business partners. They are what make us Andersen."

Jim arrived at Andersen in **1999** as vice president and general manager of the Window and Door business unit. He had enjoyed a long career in the building materials industry, including several years as the president of the largest business division of Armstrong World Industries. At Andersen, he has concentrated on increasing the company's customer focus. "Previously we were more internally focused and left the customers to others. Now the focus is on what we can do to satisfy or delight our customers," he says. "Even though we are North America's largest manufacturer of windows and doors and are viewed as the industry leader, we still manufacture only a small percentage of the units sold each year. That gives us enormous room for growth."

Already Andersen has seen results from this customer focus. The company's market share is rising — not only in the premium market segment where the company made its mark decades ago — but also in the mid-price and super-premium segments of the market. "We're clear about who our customers are, and we bring them a much wider product offering than in the past. We have to continue aligning resources on the customer, because our competitors are always trying to replace us," Jim says.

He feels very proud of the ways in which Andersen has improved its distribution system and aligned more with its customers. "We have compressed the distance between Andersen and its customers," he says. "Our old distribution system was innovative and had served us well, but it was growing obsolete. Information systems and the deregulation of the trucking industry have changed everything. When our Fulfillment Plan is completed in **2004**, customers will experience a seamless process from ordering through delivery. That will be the biggest benchmark of the success of our strategic plan."

Leading a company during a time of change demands courage and confidence. "When I leave, I want to be remembered as a president with passion for all our customers as well as the growth of our associates," he says. "My vision is to help create an innovative window and door company with the flexibility to respond to the marketplace. I hope I can be known as the president who took the company to new heights and did it by building upon the strength and principles of Andersen's first 100 years."

206

207

future

Our Values

Excellence	We will build customer trust and loyalty by understanding and caring about exceeding customer expectations for enduring quality and responsiveness.
Integrity	We take pride in our commitment to do the right thing by demonstrating fairness, integrity and high ethical standards in all of our actions.
Innovation	We will uphold our legacy of innovation and embrace change in all areas of our business as a means of attaining and sustaining leadership.
Partnership	We will cultivate successful relationships with everyone in our business circle and strengthen them through shared values, common goals and active participation.
Corporate Citizenship	We will continue our longstanding commitment to leadership in environmental stewardship and to make a positive impact in the communities in which we live and work.

Core Principles of Andersen's Relationship with Employees
— Demonstrating concern for employee well being.
— Providing opportunities for growth, development and long-term employment.
— Progressive sharing of the rewards of our success with all employees except those who are covered by a collective bargaining agreement that does not provide for their inclusion in the programs.
— Objective communication about our strategies and their impact on our business, customers and employees.
— Recognizing and rewarding performance.
— Doing "what's right." Always exercising the highest level of integrity in difficult decisions impacting the interest of employees, customers and shareholders.

Andersen Family Tree

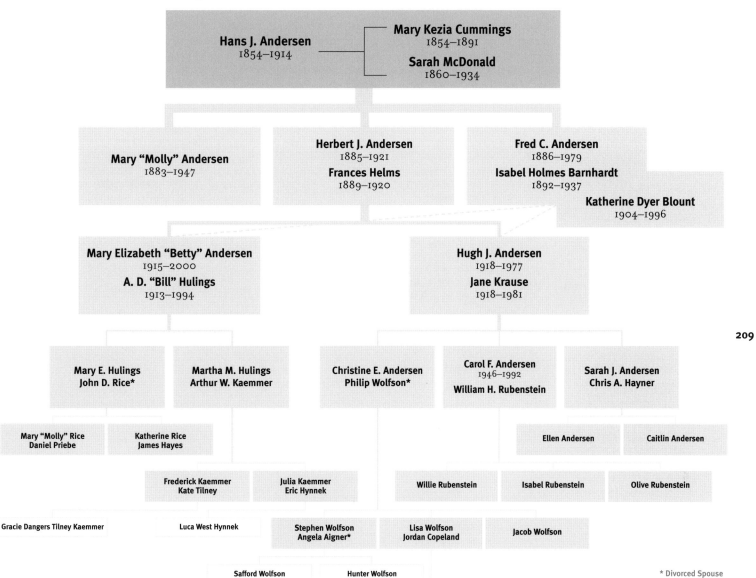

| Hans J. Andersen 1854–1914 | Mary Kezia Cummings 1854–1891 |
| | Sarah McDonald 1860–1934 |

Mary "Molly" Andersen 1883–1947

Herbert J. Andersen 1885–1921
Frances Helms 1889–1920

Fred C. Andersen 1886–1979
Isabel Holmes Barnhardt 1892–1937
Katherine Dyer Blount 1904–1996

Mary Elizabeth "Betty" Andersen 1915–2000
A. D. "Bill" Hulings 1913–1994

Hugh J. Andersen 1918–1977
Jane Krause 1918–1981

Mary E. Hulings
John D. Rice*

Martha M. Hulings
Arthur W. Kaemmer

Christine E. Andersen
Philip Wolfson*

Carol F. Andersen 1946–1992
William H. Rubenstein

Sarah J. Andersen
Chris A. Hayner

Mary "Molly" Rice
Daniel Priebe

Katherine Rice
James Hayes

Ellen Andersen

Caitlin Andersen

Frederick Kaemmer
Kate Tilney

Julia Kaemmer
Eric Hynnek

Willie Rubenstein

Isabel Rubenstein

Olive Rubenstein

Gracie Dangers Tilney Kaemmer

Luca West Hynnek

Stephen Wolfson
Angela Aigner*

Lisa Wolfson
Jordan Copeland

Jacob Wolfson

Safford Wolfson

Hunter Wolfson

* Divorced Spouse

Caleb Copeland

Acknowledgements

Different and Better—the Spirit of Andersen was a collaborative effort — the result of countless conversations over three years with many people close to Andersen. A few individuals stand out as most important to the process and who can take pride in the end result.

Chief Executive Officer Don Garofalo had the passion to capture the spirit of Andersen and the vision to tell the story from so many perspectives. It was his commitment to excellence that inspired us to do our best work.

We are grateful to President Jim Humphrey and Senior Vice President Mary Carter for their guidance on the content, for carefully reading each draft of this manuscript with keen eyes for both the big picture and the details. Their thoughtful feedback enhanced the final product.

Sincere appreciation goes to Centennial Project Manager Stacy Einck for dedicating a few years of her career to this and the entire centennial project. With creativity and clear focus, she did an outstanding job of keeping us true to our mission of documenting and celebrating Andersen's first 100 years.

We formally interviewed the Andersen family, many current and former Andersen employees, and various friends of Andersen. They not only gave their time freely and with great enthusiasm, they openly shared their memories of the past and dreams for the future. They include: Christine Andersen, Sarah Andersen, Joe Arndt, the Bell Family, Greg Benson, Bob Berg*, the Carmichael Family, Peter Clements, Loren Croone, Ross Dahlin, Phil Donaldson, Molly Ellingwood, Craig Evanich, Ed Gillstrom, Mary Gillstrom, David Harvey*, Kurt Heikkila, George Hoel, Gerry Hoel, Hap Jenson, Alan Johnson, Mike Johnson, the Judkins Family, Martha Kaemmer, Ron Kuehn, Jay Lund, Don Madsen, Hugh Madson, Margie Mattlin, Eileen Gelford Meader, Viola Gelford*, Harold Meissner, George Nelson, Phyllis Nelson, Arvid Noreen, Dick O'Brien, Et Olson*, Mary Palmer, Ray Parent, Benny Patterson, Ken Peterson, Greg Prokop, Shirley Reed, Mary Rice, Pat Riley, David and Babette Robb, Susan Roeder, May Rowland*, Carl "Doc" Schneider, Evelyn Serier, Bronson Simonet, the Speich Family, Vic Springer, Nyda Swanson, Rod Swanson, Marlene Weinberg, Arvid Wellman, and Jerry Wulf.

There are many gifted photographers and illustrators who have documented and interpreted the Andersen Corporation throughout the last 100 years. Much of their work is presented on these pages. Our deepest gratitude goes out to those professionals for their vision and the visual voice that they contributed.

We also acknowledge the late Kenneth Ruble who wrote The Magic Circle to commemorate Andersen's 75th anniversary in 1978. His documentation of the early years at Andersen was an invaluable resource to this project.

Finally, writer Jack El-Hai and designer Craig Davidson demonstrated a fierce dedication to quality that can be seen on every page of this book. Our goal to capture the spirit of Andersen was made possible by Jack's talent for telling a story, beautifully woven with color and life, and Craig's uncompromising devotion to visual flair.

To all of these people, we owe a special debt of gratitude.

Maureen McDonough
Director of
Corporate Communications

*deceased

In closing, Maureen McDonough enthusiastically served as editor on this project. She held the reigns as we passed each milestone and helped to translate conversations, interviews and documents into a compelling work of history and personal stories. Through the process, she stayed focused on the potential for excellence that is the book you now hold before you. Thank you, Maureen, for your leadership and dedication to see the vision and hear the voices that are the spirit of Andersen.

Don Garofalo
Chief Executive Officer

Page numbers in **bold** indicate photographs

Index

211

212

214

215